How to survive being

MARRIED

to a

CATHOLIC

Cartoon pages written and drawn by Michael Henesy C.Ss.R.
Remaining text by Rosemary Gallagher and Michael Henesy C.Ss.R.

Published by Redemptorist Publications
First Printed March 1986
Revised Edition November 2007

ISBN 978-0-85231-305

The ... a declaration that a book or pamphlet is considered to ... moral error. It is not implied that those who have granted the Nihil ... primatur agree with the contents.

Photographs: Shutterstock and RP Library (page 34 and 35)
Design by: Chris Nutbeen
Printed by: Cambridge University Press

Redemptorist

PUBLICATIONS

Alphonsus House, Chawton, Hampshire, GU34 3HQ
Tel. +44 (0)1420 88222 | Fax. +44 (0)1420 88805
Email. sales@rpbooks.co.uk | www.rpbooks.co.uk

INTRODUCTION

This book is primarily for anyone who's thinking of getting married to a Catholic, or who's already married to one. Its aim is to help you understand what makes Catholics tick. Not that Catholics are a different breed of human being from everyone else. You probably wouldn't be able to pick one out in a crowd...

But Catholics do hold certain beliefs which affect the way they think about themselves, other people and the world around them. Their faith has a very strong influence on the way they lead their lives. It has helped to shape their character, their ideals and their values – even if they no longer bother much with religion.

This book is designed to increase your understanding of something that's played a big part in making your partner the sort of person he or she is – and something that will continue to have a big influence. So the following pages will try to explain the meaning of the central beliefs and practices of the Catholic Church and show why they are important to your partner. But there are three things this book is **not** trying to do.

1. **This book is not** a PR job for the Roman Catholic Church. It's written as honestly as possible, and in some places points out where the Church may have had a bad influence on your partner.

* * *

2. **This book is not** setting out to prove that Catholic belief is true. It's just trying to show what it is and what it means to Catholics.

* * *

3. **This book is not** trying to persuade you to become a Catholic.

We hope that by the end you will understand your partner better and that you'll have had a few laughs along the way.

CONTENTS

Section 1
4 Catholics and religion

Section 2
8 Catholics and God

Section 3
12 Catholics and Jesus Christ

Section 4
16 Catholics and sin

Section 5
20 Catholics and redemption

Section 6
24 Catholics and the Church

Section 7
28 Introducing a Catholic word

Section 8
32 Catholics and Sunday Mass

Section 9
36 Catholics and marriage

Section 10
40 Catholics and sex

Section 11
44 Catholics and family life

Section 12
48 Catholics and prayer

Section 13
52 Portrait of a Catholic

56 Two real-life stories

57 Memo Board

58 The History Game

60 A dictionary of Catholic terms

63 Some useful addresses

People have some strange ideas about religion. Some think it's about keeping God happy:

Others think it's just something human beings cling on to, to make life more bearable:

Others think it's just harmless convention:

Still others think it's a load of boloney:

Most think they can get on perfectly well without it:

Catholics don't look at religion in any of these ways. They think religion is important because it's concerned with the deepest questions about human existence:

Questions like these cannot be answered by scientists, politicians, or economists.

Yet at the heart of human existence there lies a

Catholics aren't afraid of the word "mystery". In fact, they're very much at home with it. But when they use it they DON'T mean "something puzzling":

And they DON'T mean "something unintelligible".

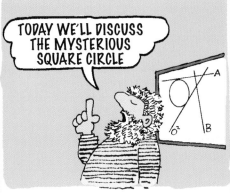

What they DO mean is something that's real, but with a meaning so deep that it can never be fathomed fully. That may sound vague, but it isn't. It's something we all experience all the time. We are surrounded by mystery whether we realise it or not. Take the natural world, for example. The more we investigate it and analyse it, the more we realise our ignorance about it. If we ask enough questions about anything we always arrive at a question that **can't** be answered.

This is especially true of the mystery that's closest to us: the mystery of the human person.

You've only got to think of someone you love to realise you can never know them completely. If you try to analyse or describe them you soon discover there's much more to them than you can put into words. Statistics, no matter how vital, just aren't enough:

Even when you think about **yourself** you realise there's a part of your being you cannot reach. You know it's there, but it's hidden from you. It is a mystery.

Now we can try summing up what we've said about religion. And the main thing to remember is that **religion** is concerned with **reality**. This is because:

1. RELIGION recognises that there is more to reality than things which can be seen and heard or weighed and measured.

2. RELIGION recognises that there is an unseen world as well as a visible one – a world of mystery which is to be found at the heart of all things.

3. RELIGION recognises that this mystery is not something vague and woolly, but something we constantly encounter in everyday experience.

Religion is concerned with exploring this mysterious and hidden side of human existence. Religion does not attempt to **explain** it. The religious quest is rather an attempt to **enter into** the mystery and **participate** in it. That is true of all religions. It is true of the Catholic faith. And it helps to explain why Catholics think religion is so important.

SOMETHING TO LEAN ON
Isn't religion just a crutch?

No, religion is just the opposite. It makes us stand on our own feet and face the reality of who we are, what we are doing here and where we are going. Religion encourages us to face the fundamental questions about life. It also provides an action-plan which enables us to make the most of our life whatever our situation.

The real crutches people lean on are things like alcohol, drugs, and astrology. These are substitutes for reality and distract us from taking responsibility for our own lives.

> **"Religion has its origins in the depth of the soul and it can be understood only by those who are prepared to take the plunge."**
>
> - Christopher Dawson

NO JOY
Religious people are always worrying about whether they'll get to heaven when they die. Doesn't that take all the enjoyment out of life?

For some people religion is a grim and gloomy business. They tend to see life as a sort of entrance exam to heaven. Obviously, if you think everything you do gains or loses you a mark, it can take the joy out of life. But not all religious people see life in that way.

Catholics believe that human beings are made for happiness – and not just happiness in the world to come. True happiness springs from love; but the love we will experience fully in heaven is not different from the love we can experience here and now. Just as our human relationships involve gradually getting to know people and reaching out to them in love, so our relationship with God grows and develops. And it begins in this life. So Catholics prefer to see life as a developing relationship with God which brings with it, here and now, a deep and lasting joy.

ROOM FOR IMPROVEMENT
Religious people don't seem to be any better than anyone else so why bother with religion?

It's a mistake to think that religion is something which "improves" people. Religion is primarily about God: his love, his creativity, his goodness and his gifts. Religion means acknowledging the reality of God, and as a result thanking him and worshipping him. Religious people don't claim to be any "better" than anyone else. A number would say they were simply better than they would be without religion. The world is a better place because some people practise religion and value God's teaching. In fact most of the great social reformers have been religious people. At times people may have used religion as an excuse for hostility and divisions, but we cannot blame religion for everything done in its name.

IN THE STARS
Is astrology compatible with religion?

Most people like to look at their horoscope in the paper; at that level astrology can be interesting and entertaining. But astrology taken seriously can never be a substitute for religion. Astrology claims to tell us what is predestined and beyond our control. We are simply "programmed" by the date and hour of our birth and the position of the stars – like human robots at the mercy of fate.

Religion is based on people's experience of a changing and evolving world and of their own life in relation to God. A religious person is not a helpless pawn. Every person can shape their own destiny and develop their full potential with the help and inspiration of God.

> **"The most beautiful experience we can have is the mysterious. It is the fundamental emotion which stands at the cradle of true art and true science."**
>
> - Albert Einstein

HAPPY AS WE ARE

My girlfriend and I are getting married because we're crazy about each other. Why should we have to bother with each other's religious beliefs?

If you are crazy about someone you want to know everything about them: their likes, their dislikes, what is important to them and what their hopes and dreams are. The religious beliefs of you and your girlfriend are part of what makes you the kind of people you are. They will form the background to many of the important decisions you will make during your lives. Before marrying someone it is essential to make sure that you know the person as well as you possibly can. Because religious belief can affect so many important aspects of married life it makes sense to share your views on it before entering into a life-long commitment.

SCIENCE AND RELIGION

Hasn't science made religion unnecessary?

There need never be any opposition between science and religion. They are both concerned with exploring the same reality, but they ask different questions about it. Science asks the question "What?"; religion asks the question "Why?"

In the past some people thought that if you asked the question "What?" long enough the question "Why?" would go away. They thought science was simply a matter of making observations and

measurements about the material world and it would only be a matter of time before everything was "explained". Einstein's theory of relativity shattered that view of science. Today scientists are much more wary about the claims they make. They are even questioning whether absolutely objective explanations are possible at all. The Danish physicist Niels Bohr has said: "Physics is not an endeavour to discover how Nature is, but an endeavour to discover what we can say about Nature."

Far from coming up with neat and tidy explanations of the universe, modern scientists are faced more and more with the mystery of it. This is reflected in the language they use in which the logic of common sense is often turned upside down.

Today many people (including some scientists) believe that religion and science are moving closer together and may be mutually helpful to each other.

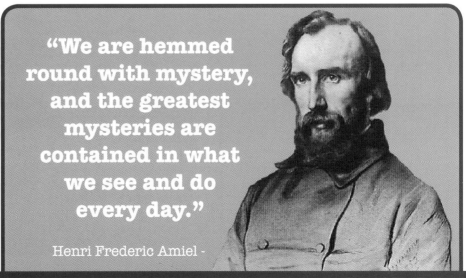

'Fraid so! In the last section we said we are surrounded by mystery. Now there's a word for the mystery which is the source of all things. The word is **God**. Unfortunately many people think of God not as the mysterious source of everything, but as an extra-powerful man in the sky.

Rather like this. . .

Or this...

Or this...

Or this...

Or this...

Or this...

The trouble with all these pictures is that they're human inventions. They're the result of people making God in their own image.

Well, partly because human beings like to have everything cut and dried. They're uneasy with anything they can't explain; or with anything that can't be weighed and measured.

We saw in the last section how the mystery of the human person defies complete analysis...

How much more is the mystery we call God beyond our comprehension? But people don't like things to be beyond their comprehension.

So people try to tie God down and make God manageable. When they do that there are bound to be distortions, and usually the distortions reflect their own fears and anxieties and guilt. That's why their pictures of God tend to come out as harsh and authoritarian.

Well, we can't avoid talking about God. But we should remember that the words we use can never capture the reality of God. Some ways of talking about God are less misleading than others. But even the best is only like a finger pointing. It's not the reality.

Good question, madam. Catholics (and other Christians) believe that

God has made **himself** known to men and women.
First he revealed himself to the Jewish people – and the story of God's dealings with them is told in the Old Testament. There we see a picture of a God who is merciful, loving and compassionate. God remains faithful to his chosen people, even when they turn away.

> When Israel was a child I loved him, and I called my son out of Egypt... I myself taught Ephraim to walk... I took them in my arms... I led them with reins of kindness, with leading-strings of love. I was like someone who lifts an infant close against his cheek; stooping down to him I gave him his food. (From the prophet Hosea)
>
> The Lord is my shepherd I shall not want; he makes me lie down in green pastures. He leads me beside still waters; he restores my soul. He leads me in paths of righteousness for his name's sake. (Psalm 23)

Christians believe that these sublime images of a loving God were brought to fulfilment in an astounding way. God not only **revealed** himself but **gave** himself to us in a person – Jesus Christ. Not simply words written down, but the Word made flesh.

Jesus doesn't tell us **about** God; he **shows** us God. That's why his life is central to Catholics and to all Christians.

PROVING GOD

It's all very well talking about God. But how do you know God exists at all? What proof is there?

It is not the purpose of this book to try to prove that any of the beliefs of Catholics are true. We are simply trying to explain what those beliefs mean to Catholics. So in answer to your question we will just give one or two indications of the sort of considerations which lead people to believe in God.

The first is a sense of wonder. If you think about the universe and your own place in it, you can't avoid the feeling that existence is very odd. You are here, but you don't really know how you got here. You certainly had nothing to do with it yourself. What is more, you continue to exist – and you don't know how you manage that either. You don't know how you breathe, or circulate your blood, or digest your food. These things just happen. When people reflect on the strangeness of existence and the wonder of it, they are led to conclude that there may be more to it than meets the eye.

Second: when we reflect on our own place in the world we realise that we are not at the mercy of blind forces. We are aware that we have freedom, and this freedom is a challenge. Our power to choose sometimes results in a struggle within ourselves. When we think about the possibility of choosing between good and evil we realise that we are measuring our actions against a standard which goes beyond purely human considerations. This leads us to believe that we may have a destiny which is more than merely human.

We can also mention people's constant quest for meaning, their hunger of heart, their desire for truth. Human beings seem to have an in-built instinct that there is something or someone who alone is capable of answering their deepest yearnings.

None of these is meant to be a watertight proof of God's existence. We've simply tried to indicate some of the lines of enquiry which lead people to believe in God.

SEVEN DAYS OF CREATION

Did God really create the world in seven days?

The Bible contains a whole range of different styles of writing and expression. There are legends, poems, history and parables, and not all of them are eyewitness accounts. The creation stories in the Book of Genesis are intended to convey the truth that the world was

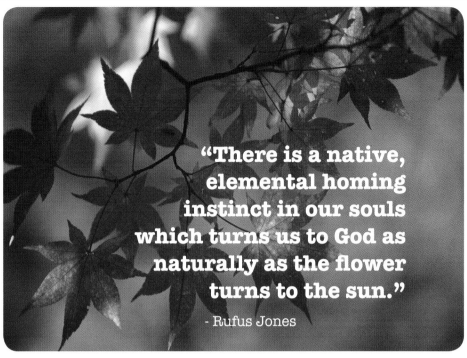

"There is a native, elemental homing instinct in our souls which turns us to God as naturally as the flower turns to the sun."

- Rufus Jones

made by God. But the details of the story express this in a poetical way. They're not meant to be an historical account of what actually happened.

SUFFERING WORLD

If God is all-powerful and all-loving why is suffering allowed in the world?

This is the commonest objection to belief in God and there is no slick answer to it. It is a question which religious thinkers in every age have grappled with and no one has yet come up with a fully satisfactory explanation. All we can do here is offer a few strands of thought which might point in the direction of a solution.

One starting point is to ask: What sort of world would it be in which suffering was totally eliminated? Clearly it would be a very different world from the one we live in now. First of all, the physical environment would have to be very different. A world in which, for example, there could be no earthquakes, no drought, no floods, no disease would have to be a physically different world from the one we live in. Is such a physically different world possible? Modern science seems to suggest that it isn't. The basic laws of physics are so finely tuned that even a minute change in them would reduce the universe to chaos. If this is the case then it looks as though the laws which make it possible for us to exist at all are the same laws which create the conditions in which suffering is possible. But even if the physical world could be changed so as to eliminate the possibility of diseases and natural disasters, that would not solve the

problem. There still remains the suffering which human beings inflict on themselves and on each other. To change that would mean changing people. Their freedom of choice would have to be destroyed, for people cannot have true freedom unless the possibility of misusing it is there. Would it be a better world if we had no free choice; if we were all programmed automatons? Would such an existence, with all suffering eliminated, be worth having?

Suffering, then, seems to be a consequence of the way things are. But it would be a mistake to think that God is indifferent to suffering, or worse – that it is deliberately inflicted by God. Christians believe that God has revealed himself in the person of Jesus Christ. And, in Jesus Christ, God has subjected himself to the consequences of the universe he has created. When Jesus died in terrible agony on the cross he showed himself to be at one with suffering humanity. He also showed that suffering can be transformed into life; that evil can be overcome by love.

This does not fully explain why there is suffering in the world but it does perhaps help us to glimpse the meaning of suffering: that it is not all a futile waste.

WISH-FULFILMENT GOD

Isn't God just a human invention? People want to believe in a supernatural being who will protect them from the harsh realities of life.

One of the greatest temptations for religious people is the tendency to invent for themselves the kind of God they would like. It is a temptation they do not always avoid. So there is some truth in what you say. But the fact that some religious people invent for themselves a comfortable God, who is a sort of insurance policy against the realities of life, does not mean that the true God does not exist.

That is one reason why Christians need constantly to re-examine their mental "picture" of God in the light of God's revelation of himself in Jesus Christ. The God Jesus shows us is not a comfortable and cosy God. He is a God who challenges us to become what we were created to be.

Fidelity to God, his Father, led Jesus to the cross, and he warned his followers that the way of faith would mean the same for them. Far from being a soft option, faith in God means fully accepting and facing the challenge of being human.

JUDGEMENT ON ME

Our child was killed in an accident. My mother says it was a judgement of God on me because I was living with my boyfriend at the time. Is she right?

No, she's not. God doesn't operate on a revenge or tit-for-tat basis. God offers forgiveness always. God sent Jesus to make this clear to us. There is no question of God counting up our failures and getting his own back.

HUMAN SUFFERING

Do not neglect your sick and elderly. **Do not** turn away from the handicapped and the dying. **Do not** push them to the margins of society. For if you do, you will fail to understand that they represent an important truth. The sick, the elderly, the handicapped and the dying teach us that weakness is a creative part of human living, and that suffering can be embraced with no loss of dignity. Without the presence of these people in your midst you might be tempted to think of health, strength and power as the only important values to be pursued in life. But the wisdom of Christ and the power of Christ are to be seen in the weakness of those who share in his sufferings.

Let us keep the sick and the handicapped at the centre of our lives. Let us treasure them and recognise with gratitude the debt we owe them. We begin by imagining that we are giving to them; we end by realising that they have enriched us.

(From a speech made by Pope John Paul II during his visit to Britain)

HELL

If God is good, why is there hell?

Our difficulties about hell arise from thinking of it as a place of "fire and brimstone". We think it's a place of torment where God sends people who disobey or who fall from favour. In reality hell is the free and deliberate refusal of God's love – and that is our choice not God's. We are invited to be with God, never forced. We retain our free will; we

cannot therefore blame God if we reject the invitation.

The imagery of "fire" in the gospel is simply a human attempt to illustrate the dreadful reality of being without God.

WHAT DOES THE BIBLE MEAN TO CATHOLICS?

Catholics have great reverence for the Bible. They believe it is the word of God. They believe it tells the story of God's revelation of himself to men and women. Each Sunday when Catholics go to Mass they hear three readings from the scriptures and they are encouraged to read the Bible privately.

What is the Bible? The Bible is not one book, it is a collection of books written by different people in different styles over a long period of time. It is divided into two main parts:
The Old Testament comes to us through the chosen race – the Jews. Written over a period of about a thousand years it tells of God's revelation of himself to the Israelite nation.
The New Testament is a collection of writings which centres on the person of Jesus Christ. It tells of his life, death and resurrection and describes the growth of the community made up of his first followers.

Who wrote the Bible? The different books of the Bible obviously required many authors and it is not always possible to say with certainty who the author of a particular book was. This is especially true in the case of some Old Testament books. But whoever the human authors were, Christians believe that God inspired them to write in such a way that

they conveyed the truth God wished them to impart. That is why the Bible is referred to as the word of God.

Is everything in the Bible true? The Bible is made up of many different kinds of writing. It contains history, prophecy, law, poetry, parables, stories and other forms of literature. When reading the Bible it is important to be aware of the kind of writing it is. Obviously poetry or parables should not be read as though they were history books. The Bible is true, but the truth it conveys is primarily religious truth. The Bible is not a text book of science or history in the modern sense and it would be a mistake to read it as though it were.

The Bible and the Church The Bible did not descend from heaven whole and complete, bound in black leather. As we have said, it was written by different people over a long period of time. It is essentially the product of a community of believers. The Old Testament arose out of the religious tradition of the Jewish people; the New Testament arose from the traditions about Jesus which were handed on and preached by the early Christian community. Because it is the product of the community, Catholics believe that the interpretation of it must be safeguarded by the authority of that same community, namely, the Church.

Imagine a little green man arriving from Mars in his spacecraft.

OK. Imagine a little **pink** man arriving from Mars in his spacecraft. What sort of questions would you want to ask him?

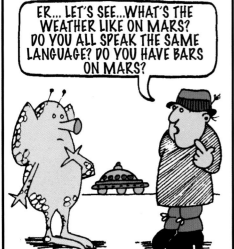

Fine. Now let's ask our little pink Martian to answer your questions.

What a pity, he can't speak English. Never mind. If he **could** make himself understood he'd give us some inside information about life on Mars. For the first time we'd have information

we couldn't have got in any other way, right?

That's OK. We've finished with him now.

The point is that some people think Jesus was a bit like that Martian: they think he came from another world (heaven) to give us inside information about God and about what God wants us to do.

This is NOT what Catholics believe about Jesus. Let's try and explain what they DO believe,

Catholics believe that Jesus was God. But they also believe he was **truly human**. He was God **and** man. In other words, he wasn't a heavenly visitor who came to earth **disguised** as a man.

And he wasn't a heavenly visitor who came to earth **pretending** to be a man. Jesus was truly human. He was born into this world. He had to learn to walk; he had to learn to read and write. He couldn't have told you that one day Columbus would discover America, and he'd have been just as amazed as anyone else in Palestine at that time if Concorde had flown over.

So Jesus wasn't an alien visitor from some higher realm with inside information to hand on. He was one of **us**. And that's why his life is so significant. In Jesus God and humanity meet. Jesus shows us that God and humankind were meant for each other.

Jesus **shows** us God in the only way we can understand – in a human life. He doesn't hand out statements

about God. He himself makes God present to us. It's as though God said:

LOOK!
THIS IS THE KIND OF GOD I AM - AND HE IS ONE OF YOU!

What, then, does the life of Jesus **tell** us about God? If you read the Gospels certain things stand out. Jesus forgives sinners; he heals the sick; he is compassionate; he is patient; he restores people to life; finally he gives his own life in love.

So the God Jesus shows us is a forgiving God, a compassionate God, a God who heals, a patient God, a life-giving God and, above all, a loving God. If we believe in Jesus we can no longer think of God as a remote, authoritarian God-in-the-sky. This God disappears for ever...

NOT AT THIS ADDRESS

Jesus shows us another face of God. His word for God is "Father". And his relationship with the God he calls Father is one of warmth, familiarity and love.

THE FATHER AND I ARE ONE

HE WHO HAS SEEN ME HAS SEEN THE FATHER

This doesn't only change our image of **God**, it changes our image of **ourselves**. We are not miserable slaves of a mighty and ruthless king. We are children of a loving God and Jesus tells **us** to call God "Father".

WHEN YOU PRAY SAY: "OUR FATHER..."

And what does it mean to be a child of God?
The life of Jesus answers that question too. He shows us how someone who is perfectly in tune with God lives. He is not fearful, timid or anxious. His relationship with God is a mature relationship. He is not divided within. He knows who he is, and he faces the demands life makes on him without dithering. He is true to the message of life he proclaims. In short, he shows us what it means to be fully human and fully alive. He is the perfect picture of a true human being.
So Jesus shows us two things:

1. He shows us what God is like in the only way we can understand: in a human life.

2. He shows us what it means to be a true human being.

So Jesus wasn't so much concerned with telling us what to **do**. He was much more concerned with showing us who we **are**. And his mission wasn't so much to make us more religious...

It was to make us more **alive**!

YIPEE!

Alive in the way he himself was alive; secure in the knowledge that he was at one with the God he called "Father".

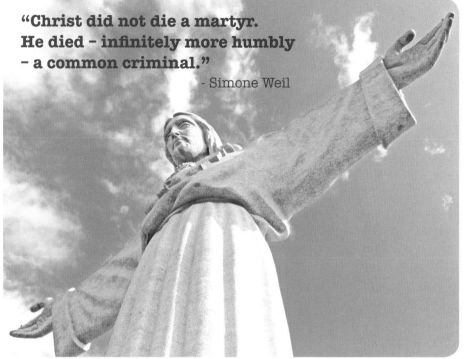

> **"Christ did not die a martyr.
> He died – infinitely more humbly
> – a common criminal."**
> - Simone Weil

FACTS ABOUT JESUS
What are the historical facts of Christ's existence?

Apart from the historical content of the Gospels there are Roman and Jewish records which mention the activities of Christ and his followers. Two of the most famous Roman writers – Pliny (writing in AD112) and Tacitus (writing in the 2nd century) – both mention the Christians and clearly regarded them as troublemakers.

The Jewish historian Josephus writes about John the Baptist. He calls John "a strange creature", but later adds, "the whole object of his life was to show evil in its true colours". In the next chapter he writes at some length about Jesus Christ as the "miracle worker". He describes his life, his death, and then writes about the "awe-inspiring signs" following the crucifixion. Josephus was born a Jew and worked for many years for the Romans as a politician, soldier and historian. He had no association with Christianity. His identity and writings are absolutely authentic and he provides an unbiased record of the reality of Christ's life and death.

YESTERDAY'S MAN
What's the point of following someone who died 2,000 years ago?

Christians do not look upon Jesus as a dead historical character – similar to someone like Julius Caesar or Napoleon. The central belief of Christians is that after his death by crucifixion, Jesus was raised to life by God, his Father.

So it is not accurate to say that Christians follow someone who died 2,000 years ago. Christians believe that Jesus is alive now and through his Spirit still has an influence on the lives of his friends and followers.

Over the last 2,000 years millions of people have experienced the living presence of Jesus, and they have discovered the point of following him by experiencing the difference he makes to their lives.

RESURRECTION
How can anyone believe that Jesus Christ came back to life after dying on the cross?

Strictly speaking, Christians do not believe that Jesus "came back to life". They believe that God, his Father, raised Jesus to a new kind of life – a life which is eternal and which death can no longer touch. If he had "come back to life" he would still be subject to death because death is an inevitable part of this present life. But Christians believe that the risen body of Jesus can never die again. He has conquered death. That is why Christians say that Jesus is alive now.

The foundation for belief in the resurrection rests on the witness of the first disciples of Jesus. They saw him after his resurrection and ate and drank with him. This experience of meeting the risen Lord transformed them. They became his witnesses – proclaiming that Jesus who was crucified had been raised to life. Many of those first witnesses were put to death for their belief.

The resurrection of Jesus is a unique event. We cannot describe it or say how it happened. Nor can it be proved scientifically. We can only say it did happen. For 2,000 years Christians have proclaimed their faith in the resurrection of Jesus because they experience his abiding presence in their own lives.

TOO MANY CHURCHES
If Christians are followers of Jesus why are they divided into so many different Churches? Shouldn't they all belong to one Church?

The main divisions between the Christian Churches date from the 11th century (when the Eastern and Western Churches split off from each other) and from the Reformation in the 16th century – which led to the divisions between

Catholics and Protestants. The reasons for these divisions are complex and we cannot go into them in detail here. Some have their origin in doctrinal differences. But politics and prejudice also played a part.

Today nearly all Christians agree that disunity is a scandal and that everything possible must be done to overcome it. And much is being done, both at an official level and among ordinary Christians. For example, it is becoming more and more common for members of different Churches to worship together and to work together on projects which express Christian concern. Suspicion and misunderstandings are gradually being broken down and Christians are much more willing than they once were to recognise the truth and the value in each other's traditions. But it is a slow process. The divisions of centuries cannot be healed overnight, and firmly held beliefs cannot be brushed aside as being of no importance.

The Catholic Church is firmly committed to the search for unity among Christians. In England and Wales discussions have been established between the Catholic and Anglican Churches, and between Catholics and Methodists.

Every year there is a week of prayer for Christian unity which all the Christian Churches take part in. It usually takes place from 18th to 25th January.

LIFE AFTER DEATH

When my aunt's husband died she made contact with him through a medium. Is this proof of life after death?

Many claims are made about what happens at seances and some spiritualist meetings where there is a medium. Sometimes people are taken advantage of or manipulated, and great suffering ensues, especially when people are distressed. Someone like your aunt, recently bereaved, is particularly vulnerable in her loneliness and sadness. The Catholic Church does not approve of such meetings.

For Christians, faith in Jesus Christ is the basis of their assurance that there is life after death.

MARY THE MOTHER OF JESUS

The place of Mary in Catholic belief is often misunderstood. Catholics do not worship her and they do not assign to her any power which belongs to God alone.

Catholics honour Mary because of the part she played in co-operating with God to bring about the salvation of the human race. God chose her to be the mother of the Saviour. Through her God entered human history. No greater dignity could be conferred on any human being. But this dignity was not forced upon her. It depended on her acceptance. The first chapter of St Luke's Gospel describes how she responded to God's call: "I am the handmaid of the Lord," said Mary, "let what you have said be done to me." Because of her faith in responding to God's call Catholics see Mary as the model of all Christian discipleship. As the mother of Jesus she was the first to commit herself to him and to his service. So she can truly be called the first Christian. Catholics look upon Mary as their spiritual mother because of the great things God has done through her.

THE GOD JESUS REVEALS

Mr Berkowitz, a Jewish tailor, was out walking one day when he was run over at a busy crossing. A crowd gathered and a Catholic priest who happened to be passing pushed his way through to see if he could assist the dying man. The priest knelt beside Mr Berkowitz and whispered, "Do you believe in God the Father, God the Son and God the Holy Spirit?" Mr Berkowitz raised his eyes to heaven and said: "I'm dying and he asks me riddles."

Mr Berkowitz's difficulty with the Christian doctrine of the Trinity (the doctrine that there are three persons in one God) is shared by many people – including some Christians themselves. It looks like a mathematical puzzle. How can three be one and one be three? But Jesus did not reveal to us a puzzling doctrine, he spoke of a reality which he himself experienced. Here are some of the things he said:

"I and the Father are one."

"The Father is greater than I."

"To have seen me is to have seen the Father."

"...the Holy Spirit, whom the Father will send in my name, will teach you everything and remind you of all I have said to you."

Catholics (and other Christians) believe that Jesus revealed something of immense importance to us about the nature of God. He revealed that God does not stand monolithic and alone. Within the one Godhead there is a movement and relation. That is why we can say "God is love".

This has important implications for us as God's creatures. For we are made in God's image. That means we are made for relationship, for communion, for love. So the revelation of God as Father, Son and Holy Spirit tells us something about our own destiny. We are created to share in the community of love which is the living God.

We are not in the realm of "riddles" here, we are in the realm of mystery. And mystery cannot be put into words. The doctrine of the Trinity is an attempt to express something which cannot be expressed. Words necessarily fail; but for Christians the reality remains.

SIN, EH! COR, NOW WE'RE REALLY GETTING DOWN TO IT

Sorry to disappoint you, but we'd better warn you right away that sin is a pretty boring subject.

BORING? BUT I ALWAYS THOUGHT IT WAS TO DO WITH A BIT OF THE OLD... WINK-WINK, NUDGE-NUDGE... KNOW WHAT I MEAN?

Pardon?

YOU KNOW...FUN AND THAT! SIN AND FUN GO TOGETHER DON'T THEY?

All right, let's see if they do. Which of these two roads would you take to get the most fun?

This way for

Greed
Envy
Deceit
Cruelty
Hatred
Prejudice
Revenge
Selfishness
Injustice
Exploitation
Resentment
Lust
Avarice

This way for

Love
Truth
Trust
Justice
Kindness
Integrity
Fidelity
Generosity
Honesty
Respect
Forgiveness
Gentleness
Compassion

...ER

Well?

HMM... I SEE WHAT YOU'RE GETTING AT. THERE'S NOT MUCH FUN TO BE HAD BY TAKING THE LEFT FORK

Right. And that's one of the most important things to grasp about sin as Catholics understand it. **It is harmful to human beings.**

HEALTH WARNING
SINNING CAN SERIOUSLY DAMAGE YOURSELF

I'VE NEVER THOUGHT OF IT LIKE THAT. I THOUGHT SIN WAS TO DO WITH BREAKING GOD'S LAWS

Well it **is**. But that's just another way of saying the same thing. Remember: God is on our side. So the laws he gives us are for our benefit – to stop us getting into a mess. Just look at some of them...

> You shall not kill
> You shall not steal
> You shall not commit adultery
> You shall not covet your neighbour's goods
> You shall not bear false witness against your neighbour

Commandments like these do not restrict our freedom. They stand like a **No Entry** sign on a road that leads to human misery.

Misery   Happiness

In other words, the commandments are made for **our** sake. We're not made for the sake of the commandments.

YOU MEAN THEY'RE NOT A SORT OF TEST TO SEE IF WE'LL OBEY GOD'S AUTHORITY?

Certainly not.

WELL WHY DO PEOPLE BREAK THEM, THEN? IF SIN HARMS US WHY DO WE KEEP ON DOING IT?

Good question. And not an easy one to answer. In fact it's impossible to answer completely. But here's a hint...

FIRST: Have you ever seen a dog in a dilemma?

DECISIONS, DECISIONS... ALL THE TIME DECISIONS

SLABBY MEAT   MEATY SLABS

CAN'T SAY I HAVE THEY JUST GO BY INSTINCT, DON'T THEY?

Right. People, on the other hand, are faced with choices and decisions all the time.

HAVE YOU GOT THE SAME THING IN NAVY BLUE?

But the choices we make aren't only concerned with trivial preferences. We also have the freedom to choose how we'll live our lives...

Choices like these are not easy to make. Our whole future happiness may depend on what we decide. And naturally, our happiness is very important to us. So we tend to choose what we think will make us happy. But we're not always very good at it. In the story, King Midas thought it would make **him** happy if everything he touched turned to gold. Then he kissed his daughter and...

We've all got a bit of the King Midas in us. We tend to want to satisfy our immediate desires. We want instant happiness. And sometimes that **blinds** us to the consequences of our actions.

At other times we can see quite clearly that a particular choice will lead to harmful consequences – for ourselves and for other people. But we still go ahead and make the harmful choice.

Choices of this kind are impossible to explain. They are the result of a quirk in human nature that we all experience but are powerless to get rid of. To put it in Christian terms: we have to live with a "fallen" human nature.

Not if it bothers you. All we're trying to point out is that human beings have to live with inner conflict. We are **divided** selves.

We may not know **why** we are like that, or how we got like that, but we do know that's the way we **are**. We **are** capable of choosing to take that left fork, even though we know it's a road that leads to nowhere. And frequently we **do** take it...

So sin, strictly speaking, is an irrational act. It separates us from the things we **really** want.

Sin separates us from the people we love because we can't be at one with them if we constantly hurt them or use them.
Sin separates us from ourselves because it destroys our sense of self-respect.
Sin separates us from life because it makes us closed-in and self-centred.
Sin separates us from God because God wants what's best for us and we've chosen what's worst for us.

There's no human answer to sin. But there **is** a divine answer. It's the answer Jesus gave to those who acknowledged their sinfulness.

God's readiness to forgive is the only possible answer to sin. Where sin separates, forgiveness reunites. Forgiveness brings hope to sinners, it restores their dignity, it assures them that they are accepted. Forgiveness enables people to live again – free from anxiety and guilt.

Well, God is ready to **forgive** you again and again... and again... and again...

17

NO HARM DONE

How can something which doesn't harm anyone be a sin?

It is impossible to sin and not hurt someone, even if that someone is only yourself. Pollution within the environment is often the result of activities which were once thought to be harmless. It is the same with sin. It deforms, warps or poisons what is good. Therefore even if no one else is involved, sin damages your **own wholeness** and goodness. And that is just as serious as hurting someone else.

NOT ALL BAD

How can you tell whether someone is really wicked? Surely most people are a mixture of good and bad?

No one is so wicked that there's no possibility of change in their lives. You are right, most people **are** a mixture of good and bad. We're conscious of being divided within ourselves. We want to do what is good and right but very often we act in ways that are harmful to ourselves and other people. So there isn't always a clear-cut distinction between the left-hand fork and the right-hand fork as in the illustration on page 17. Most of the time the two roads seem to criss-cross each other. Sometimes we're on one, sometimes on the other and sometimes we seem to be on both at the same time.

Christians try to walk the right-hand road, but they are well aware that they keep making detours onto the left-hand road. When they do that they first of all need to realise they're going off in the wrong direction, and then they need to get back on the right road as soon as possible. That is what the word "repentance" means: with God's help, getting back on the right road again. We need to do this throughout our lives. There's no one who can truthfully say, "I'm on the right road now and I'll never wander off it again."

DO AS YOU LIKE

Christians say that God will always forgive your sins. But doesn't that make sin meaningless? If he always forgives, it means you can do as you like.

Think of a teenager who's on hard drugs. His parents may be very angry that he's allowed himself to get into this state. They will certainly disapprove of his actions and will want him to stop taking drugs. They will also be very distraught at the harm he is doing to himself. But they will go on loving him. They will give him all the support they can – even if he finds it impossible to give up drugs, or keeps slipping back into taking them after receiving treatment to wean him off them.

Their love, support and forgiveness do not mean they think his drug-taking doesn't matter. Quite the opposite! They go on loving him because they want what is best for him. They don't want him to go on destroying himself.

Sin is a bit like drug-taking. It, too, is self-destructive. When God forgives our sin, and goes on forgiving it, he is acting rather like the parents of the drug addict – only with infinitely greater love, compassion and patience. He is saying: "Please do not destroy yourself; let me love you back to wholeness."

CONFESSION TO A PRIEST

Why do Catholics have to confess their sins to a priest? Why can't they confess to God directly?

Catholics **can** confess their sins to God directly, and they frequently do so. They are encouraged to examine their consciences daily and to express sorrow in their own hearts for any sins they have committed. They are **obliged** to confess to a priest only if they know they have committed a serious sin by which they have deliberately cut themselves off from God. However, most Catholics go to the Sacrament of Reconciliation periodically even though they may have nothing as serious as that to confess.

There are three main reasons for confessing to a priest in this way.

First: Jesus gave his apostles the authority to forgive sins, and Catholics believe that this authority has been handed on to bishops and priests throughout the Church's history. This is consistent with God's way of communicating with us – through visible signs. We are flesh-and-blood human beings and we communicate in a physical way. Through the priest God allows us to hear that our sins are forgiven. (See section seven.)

Second: Confession does not only reconcile us with God, it also reconciles us with the Church. Sin harms the whole community of believers. Just as two people having a row at a party put a damper on the whole gathering, so the sin of a member of the Body of Christ, the Church, has repercussions for the whole body of believers. Confession to a priest, as the Church's representative, is an expression of our sorrow and our desire to be reconciled with our fellow Christians.

Third: The priest is often able to offer counsel, advice and encouragement to the penitent in the light of the penitent's own particular circumstances.

INSIDE STORY

If my wife goes to confession will the priest find out all about ME?

When your wife goes to confession she is seeking reconciliation with God from whom she has turned away through her own sinfulness. The ways in which she has rejected God's love are the matters she will mention in confession. She will acknowledge these failings as honestly as she can. She may also seek help and advice from the priest about overcoming particular faults she recognises within herself.

When Catholics go to confession they look into their **own** hearts and examine their **own** behaviour. A priest would actively discourage a penitent who tried to tell him about other people's faults and failings.

SIN ON THE BRAIN

The Catholic Church seems to be preoccupied with sin. Will my Catholic partner be always worrying about it?

The Catholic Church has a realistic attitude to sin, not a preoccupation with it. And that goes for most Catholics, too. Catholics acknowledge that a tendency towards sin is an inevitable part of being human. No one can claim they always do what is right and good. We are all aware that we sometimes act in ways which we ourselves disapprove of. For example, we inflict hurt on others, or act in ways that are mean, selfish or cruel.

Catholics recognise that in their sinfulness they are at one with the rest of humanity. So their sin doesn't make them anxious or guilt-ridden. Within the Church they know they have access to the only answer to sin: the forgiveness of Christ. They acknowledge their sin and are sorry for it. That is enough. They don't need to be constantly worried about it.

SIN AND SEX

Why is the Church so concerned about sexual sin?

The Church isn't any more concerned about sexual sin than any other kind of sin. All sin is destructive and damaging to ourselves and others. Our sexuality is so closely linked with our deepest emotional and psychological needs that its misuse or abuse can be especially harmful. Our sexuality is also one of the most powerful forces within us, so we are particularly vulnerable in this area.

Through our sexuality we can enrich, affirm and strengthen one another; we can also destroy, undermine and crush one another with its misuse. For these reasons the Church does speak out on questions of sexual morality for it sees sex as one of God's most precious gifts.

It is probably true to say that through the physical union of sexual intercourse two people who are spiritually one in God may know the closest experience of heaven possible on this earth. The Church values this possibility and guards it. That is why the Church does not want us to squander such a gift.

OBEYING THE RULES

The Catholic Church seems to have so many rules. If I marry a Catholic will I be expected to obey them?

No, you will not: though any support or encouragement you feel you can give to your Catholic partner in the practice of his or her faith will be very welcome.

OFFENCE

How is God offended by my sin?

God isn't "offended" by our sin in the way we would take offence. Sin eats into us, it numbs our sensitivity, so that we become less responsive to God's call to love. The result is that we begin to grow away from God, which is the opposite of God's wish for us.

Parents who see their children spoiling their chances in life are not offended, only saddened on behalf of the child because of the opportunities the child is missing.

WHAT HAPPENS WHEN CATHOLICS GO TO CONFESSION

"Confession" is a misleading way of describing the Sacrament of Reconciliation even though it's the word Catholics themselves most frequently use. It gives the impression that the verbal confession of sins is the central and most important part of the sacrament. This is not the case. The confession of sins is only one element in a process which enables a person to meet Christ and respond to his call to repentance.

Nowadays there is a good deal of flexibility in the way the Sacrament of Reconciliation (a more accurate title) is celebrated. So it is not possible to describe one form of it which is always followed. For example, the confessional box which enables the penitent to remain anonymous doesn't need to be used. Provision is now made for penitents to meet the priest "face to face" if they wish. Many Catholics prefer this because it makes the sacrament more personal and makes it easier to talk over problems.

The elements which make up the rite of reconciliation are these:

• **Preparation:** By prayer and a careful reflection on their way of life the penitents call to mind their failures as Christians; express sorrow for them in their heart; and resolve to amend their lives.

• **Greeting:** When the person enters the confessional box or the room where the sacrament is celebrated the priest welcomes them warmly and invites them to sit or kneel.

• **Invitation to trust:** Priest and penitent make the sign of the cross together and the priest says a few words in which he invites the penitent to trust in God's mercy.

• **Introduction:** The penitent may now tell the priest anything which may be relevant. For example, whether married or single, how long it is since the last confession etc.

• **Scripture reading:** If there is time the priest or penitent may read a suitable passage from scripture which draws attention to God's mercy and his call to repentance.

• **Confession of sins:** Penitents tell their sins to the priest simply and humbly. The priest may offer counsel or advice or talk over any special problems the penitent may have.

• **Giving a penance:** The priest asks the penitent to perform some act of penance to show willingness to make up for the past. The penance may take the form of prayer, self-denial, or acts of service to others.

• **Act of sorrow:** The penitent says a short prayer which expresses sorrow for sin and resolution to seek amendment of life.

• **Absolution:** The priest extends his hand over the penitent and pronounces the words of absolution.

• **Conclusion:** The priest says a short prayer expressing praise and thanks to God and tells the penitent to go in peace.

"The deepest need of man is the need to overcome his separateness, to leave the prison of his aloneness." - Erich Fromm

This is the story of Fred. Fred was a quiet, gentle sort of person, with a nice wife called Sue and two lovely children.

But Fred had always been unsure of himself; he felt deep down that he wasn't good enough for Sue. All his friends had better jobs, better cars, and better houses than Fred. When with them he felt like a nonentity and secretly envied them their confidence and their success.

Then one day Fred was offered a new job.

You've got potential, Fred. You could go far with our company. You could be Somebody — a Top Executive.

Fred rather fancied himself as a Top Executive... So he said...

I'll take it

At last I'll be Somebody.

Fred was determined to succeed in his new job, so he applied himself.

He worked hard...

He kept well in with the boss...

He stayed late in the office...

And he took work home at the week-ends...

Sue and the children saw less and less of him...

Mummy, who's that strange man?

But when Sue tackled him about it Fred said:

I've got to get ahead. I want to be Somebody. And I'm doing it all for you. You should be grateful.

So he went on applying himself. He got promotion. And that meant he had more work and more responsibility. So he worked even harder...
And he stayed even later at the office...
And he took loads of work home at weekends...
And his family saw even less of him.

Who was that?

When Sue complained he said:

Think of the salary increase I've had. Soon we'll be able to move into a bigger house.

But I like it here

A man in my position should be moving up-market. This dump is no longer in line with my status.

So they moved to a bigger house. Then they got a bigger car, which was also more in line with Fred's status. And a boat, because that was in line with his status too.
But when the children said...

Can you take us to the seaside and sail the boat, Daddy?

Fred always said...

I'm too busy. I've got a lot of work to do

So they never went out in the boat. But it was in the front drive for all to see.

Fred went on working very hard. But gradually the long hours and the need to meet targets began to take their toll. He began to get irritable and morose. When Sue complained, Fred said:

Can't you stop your nagging, you old bag!

Soon they were all very unhappy – especially Fred. Only the thought of being **Somebody** kept him going. And he worked harder to achieve it. The harder he worked, the more irritable and unhappy he became. Even his friends noticed the deterioration. They advised him to take a nice long holiday. But Fred said:

I can't. There's too much to do. I can't leave it.

So although he felt terrible all the time and his wife and children hardly dared speak to him, he went grinding on. Until one day two things happened. Sue and the children walked out...

And Fred collapsed with a perforated ulcer. In hospital Fred had time to think for the first time for years...

How did I get into this mess? I'm stuck in here, I've lost Sue and the kids, and I don't know what to do next. I might as well be dead.

But he hadn't lost Sue and the kids. When they heard he'd been rushed into hospital, they rushed to see him.

Fred...are you all right?

No... I'm in a mess. I wanted to be Somebody and now I'm Nobody.

Then Sue said quietly...

You're Somebody to us, Fred. You always have been and you always will be.

Yes! You're our Dad!

This was news to Fred.

You mean you don't mind if I'm not a Top Executive?

I love you, Fred, not your position in the Company or your salary.

At that moment Fred's image of himself as a Top Executive went...

POP!

And for the first time in his life he realised it was OK just to be himself.

I'm Fred

When he came out of hospital Fred handed in his notice and took a much more modest job. It meant a big cut in his salary and saying goodbye for ever to being a Top Executive. It also meant moving back to a smaller house and selling the posh car and the boat. But before selling the boat, Fred took Sue and the kids out for a sail in it.

THE END

Christians have a word for what happened to Fred: they call it "Redemption". To be redeemed means to be made whole; to be made truly and fully yourself. Fred's problem was that he couldn't accept himself for what he was. He felt inferior. So he tried to substitute another "self" — one he thought he **could** accept: Fred the Top Executive.

THERE'S MORE

But Fred wasn't cut out for that kind of life and instead of bringing self-fulfilment it brought self-destruction. Yet in the midst of destruction Fred saw the light. Through the love of Sue and the children he learned to recognise and accept the true Fred. The Top Executive died, and Fred himself began to live.

Fred's story is everybody's story. Not in its details but in what it reveals. Very few people are completely whole. The vast majority are wounded in some way.

There aint nuthin' wrong with me!

Nearly everyone lives with fears, anxieties, phobias which prevent them from being fully alive and fully themselves. Like Fred, many people try to make up for it by substituting something else. Anything will do: booze, drugs, sex, betting, wealth, hard work, politics, religion... The thing itself may be harmless, or even good; but when it's used as a substitute for real living it can be lethal.

You've only got to look at my face to realise I'm a very integrated person with no hang-ups at all

Many people go through their whole lives relying on substitutes. Others, like Fred, are more fortunate. Something happens which forces them to face reality. In Fred's case it was illness and the fear of losing his family. For other people it might be failure, disappointment, dissatisfaction, unhappiness or any one of a number of things.
It's a painful experience realising that you've been going down a blind alley.

But it's the first step on the road to recovery.

I'm getting out of here

The second step is realising that you are accepted for what you are. Through Sue's acceptance Fred learned to accept his own limitations. He was valued for himself. He learned to live without anxiety. He was a new man.

You can say that again

Christians recognise a pattern of death and rebirth in all this. They learn it from Jesus. Jesus was the true, perfect man, he lived his life fully and completely. He brought this fullness of life to people he met. By love, warmth and friendship he made broken people whole. Jesus treated no one as a write-off. He deliberately mixed with the outcasts and sinners of society and through restoring their dignity and self-esteem enabled them to live again.

I have come that they may have life and have it to the full.

But there was a price to pay. The true man, the complete man, stood as a challenge to the pious, the narrow-minded, the guardians of conventional religion. They resented him and they resisted him. Eventually they had him killed.

Yet his death was not failure but fulfilment. Not an end but a beginning. Jesus broke through the chains of death and rose to a new life – a life that death could never touch again. He lives that life now and he still offers it to the world – just as he offered it to the outcasts and sinners of Palestine.

How do we receive it? Well, our friend Fred received it when he discovered he could be himself. For there's nothing vague about the life Jesus offers. We experience it whenever we're saved from the destructive elements in our lives and begin to see a new path stretching out before us. Very often the agent of new life is another person. Their love releases us and gives us new hope.

You're Somebody to us, Fred. You always have been and you always will be.

Yes! you're our Dad!

This is the redeeming love of Jesus Christ at work in the world.

HELP YOURSELF

Why does anyone need to be redeemed? The only way to improve yourself is by self-discipline.

If you have any doubt about humanity's need of redemption you need look no further than the news on TV or the front page of your daily paper. A moment's thought will convince you that we live in a wounded world; a world in which people are at odds with each other and in which greed and selfishness seem to thrive. The numbing thing about the evil we see all around us is that we as individuals seem powerless to do anything about it.

But the disease is not only outside us. If we're at all honest we recognise the seeds of wickedness within ourselves. We are divided selves. We may want what is good; we may desire to be fully integrated people who express our wholeness in love and care and service. But we also know we often fall short of that. Fear cripples us and we opt for self-interest. We are tainted with the malaise that inflicts the whole of humanity – and no matter how hard we try, no matter how much self-discipline we apply, we cannot get rid of that inner conflict.

That is why Christians believe that we need to be redeemed. We need to be shown that the creative power of love can meet the evil in the world and overcome it. That is what Jesus achieved by his death and resurrection.

SAVIOUR

As a Christian I accept Jesus Christ as my personal Saviour. My Catholic husband doesn't seem to think this is enough. Why?

It is fundamental Catholic teaching that salvation comes through Jesus Christ alone and that the salvation he offers can be freely accepted by individuals. So Catholics **also** accept Jesus Christ as their personal Saviour.

But the way your husband thinks of this probably differs in emphasis from the way you think of it. Catholics recognise the importance of a person's initial conversion and commitment to Christ, but they do not see this as a decision which is made only once in a lifetime. They look upon faith very much as a way of life, as something which grows and develops, rather than something which is given whole and complete at one particular moment.

So while Catholics do accept Jesus as their personal Saviour, they also emphasise the importance of living out their commitment in daily life – helped by God's grace and the guidance of the Holy Spirit. In other words, they see their commitment to Christ as something which is constantly renewed, not something which happens only once.

AFTER DEATH

The Church is sometimes accused of persuading people to become believers with promises of "pie in the sky when you die". It is an accusation which is not easy to refute. Life after death cannot be scientifically proved. Still less is it possible to describe what a future life will be like. On these matters Christians have to be content to live by faith, not by absolute certainty.

The foundation for that faith is Jesus Christ. Christians believe that the "fullness of life" which Jesus came to bring cannot be completely realised in the limited confines of this world. We, like Jesus himself, are destined to break through the chains of death and live in the closest union with God for ever.

But this destiny is not forced upon us. If we wish we can reject God and choose to live apart from him. This, in essence, is what hell means. Life with God is heaven.

We cannot describe what either heaven or hell is like and it is futile to speculate. The Bible uses imagery and metaphor to talk about them, but we should never take these as literal descriptions.

Nearly all Catholics, at some time in their lives, get just a bit fed up with the Catholic Church.

They get fed up with it when it seems to concentrate too much on rules and regulations.

Or when it appears to lock people up in fear and guilt.

Or when it tries to destroy individual responsibility...

Throughout its history the Church has been guilty of all these things – and much worse. It's been guilty of cruelty, intolerance, power-seeking, persecution and injustice. When the Church shows these symptoms people are **right** to kick against it. When it shows these symptoms the Church is failing in its central task. It is claiming for itself an authority it does not possess – a false authority.

Throughout its history the Church has been the means through which millions of people in every age, and of every class and every race, have come to know Jesus Christ and his life-giving message. From its ranks the Church has produced individuals who are universally recognised for their outstanding goodness and holiness. People like. . .

St Paul... St Francis of Assisi... and, in our own time, **Mother Teresa of Calcutta** and **Pope John Paul II.**

When the Church is deeply aware of its mission to be a **sign** of Jesus in this world, and to hand on his message of love and forgiveness, then it **is** fulfilling its task. And this is where its **true** authority lies.

If you're married to a Catholic you'll inevitably run up against both these faces of the Catholic Church. On the one hand you'll meet Catholics (both clerical and lay) who are self-seeking, vindictive, intolerant, petty, hypocritical, or just plain cracked.

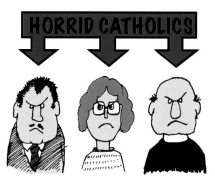

But you'll also meet Catholics who have a deep faith, who try to love God and their fellow human beings, whose lives are a genuine manifestation of the love and compassion of Jesus Christ.

You shouldn't be surprised at these two very different faces of the Catholic Church.
The Church isn't a kind of club for people who are interested in religion. And you don't have to pass a test in moral uprightness before you can join...

The Church is made up of **people**... ordinary human beings who don't have a magic formula for being good. The Church is the community of believers – all of them, not just popes, bishops and priests. It's a community of people on a voyage of discovery. Together they're trying to move closer to God; they're trying to find out more about themselves and their place in the world; they're trying to follow in the footsteps of Jesus; they're trying to learn how best to serve their fellow men and women.

Yes! They don't believe they've got all the answers. They make a lot of mistakes both individually and collectively. But no matter how much they fail to live up to the teaching of Christ, this community – the Church – somehow goes on.

And as it goes on it **points** – not to itself but to Jesus Christ.

Catholics believe that the Church is not simply a human institution. The life of the Church does not depend on human organisational skills. The life of the Church springs from the Spirit of Christ living in the hearts of all its members.
Jesus is not dead, he is alive. And the Spirit which was the driving force in his life has now been released on all his followers. This Spirit of Jesus is what gives the Church its life, its motivation, its heart.

At times in the Church's history some of its members have been unfaithful to the Spirit of God. But the Spirit always remains faithful to the Church. That's why, in spite of its many failings, the Church continues to be a sign of Christ's presence in the world, and continues to proclaim his message of love, forgiveness, human dignity, joy, hope and peace.

GO IT ALONE
Why do you have to belong to a Church to follow Christ?

Because belonging to the Church seems to be the nearest we can get on this earth to doing what Jesus Christ asked us to do. He talked about loving our neighbour as ourselves. If we don't mix with each other we cannot even get to know our neighbour. He asked us to pray together. He talked about many being united in "one body". We need this Christian community to help us to find Christ in ourselves and in each other.

BISHOPS OF THE WORLD UNITE!

The Catholic Church is not a one-man show. The Pope has a special role of leadership but he does not exercise it alone. The bishops, as successors of the apostles, are also leaders within the Church.

All the bishops together form what is called "The College of Bishops". In union with the Pope they are responsible for preserving and teaching the Catholic faith. Normally this is carried out by each bishop in his own locality, where he is a focus for unity and leadership. But occasionally all the bishops of the world gather together for a General Council of the Church.

There have been twenty-one such Councils in the Church's history. (They are sometimes called "Ecumenical Councils" – meaning they represent the Church world-wide.) The last General Council was held in the Vatican from 1962 to 1965. It is referred to as the Second Vatican Council – sometimes abbreviated to "Vatican II". Many wide-ranging changes in the Catholic Church stemmed from this Council.

> "Christ cannot live his life today in this world without our mouth, our eyes, without our going and coming, without our heart. When we love, it is Christ loving through us. This is Christianity."
>
> - Cardinal Suenens

HISTORICAL HORRORS
Looking at some of the terrible things which have been done in the history of the Church, how can it claim to be guided by God?

The Church is made up of saints and sinners and there is something of both in everyone. It is not only those who are already "perfect" who belong to the Church. Everyone is called to be perfect but most people have some way to go.

The history of the Church is a history of people – as varied as people can be. There are stories of saints and stories of sinners, of good and bad. Sometimes the bad have held authority in the Church and scandalous things have been done in its name. It has been said that the fact of the Church's survival, despite the wickedness of some of its leaders, is a sign in itself that the Church must be from God.

PRIESTS AND MARRIAGE
Why don't priests get married? If they had to keep a wife and family they'd be much more understanding of people's problems.

Catholic priests remain unmarried so that they'll be free to love and serve the whole family of God. But you may be right. If they **were** married they might understand some things better. But getting married is no **guarantee** that you'll understand other people's problems. Sometimes a detached view can be much more valuable.

The fact that a priest is unmarried does not mean he is somehow sealed-off from problems and difficulties. He is human the same as everyone else and, like everyone else, has to cope with difficulties in relationships, clashes of temperament and so on.

Priests who work in parishes are not usually very well-off financially – so they're well aware of what it means to have to make ends meet, too.

ESCAPIST NUNS
It doesn't seem human for women to lock themselves away in convents. Isn't this a form of escapism?

It would be escapism if they were running away from, say, a broken love affair or wanted to avoid facing up to the responsibilities of adult life. But most women who join a religious order do so because they feel a special call to love and serve God. By committing their lives to God as religious sisters they are making a public statement that they are willing to work in the service of their fellow men and women for the rest of their lives. Far from "running away" they are saying "we are always available".

This is also true of women who feel called to enter "enclosed" religious orders. Although they have little contact with the outside world they spend their lives praying for people in all walks of life. If you ever have the opportunity to visit an enclosed convent you'll quickly revise your opinion that this way of life is in some way "inhuman".

HYPOCRISY

Catholics are hypocrites. Why do they pretend to be better than the rest of us?

It is surprising how many people share your views. Perhaps it is because Catholics lay great stress on going to Mass and confessing their sins to a priest. In fact Catholics don't pretend to be better than anyone else. If you ask them, most will probably say that they consider themselves no better and at times worse.

The idea that Catholics are morally superior to anyone else is false. The Catholic Church is in reality like a band of pilgrims on a journey towards the God who loves them.

CATHOLIC KNOW-ALLS

Why does the Catholic Church think it's got all the answers?

Sometimes spokespeople for the Church may give that impression. In fact the Church only claims to have the answers to certain essential questions about Christ and his message of salvation.

These answers are based on the words of Christ, the words of the apostles and the promises of Christ to guide those who serve him and his Church.

WHO'S WHO?

The organisation of the Catholic Church seems very complicated, with the Pope, Cardinals, Archbishops, Bishops, Priests, Monks and Nuns etc. How do they all fit together?

The part of the Church's organisation you are most likely to come into contact with is the parish. This is led by the parish priest – sometimes alone, sometimes with the assistance of one or more priests who are called curates. Parishes vary in size. A village or country town will probably have only one parish, whereas large cities are divided into numerous parishes. The parishes in a particular area form a diocese – and each diocese is under the care of a bishop. Several dioceses form a province – with an archbishop in charge. The Bishop of Rome – the Pope – is the head of the bishops and of the whole Church. Cardinals are appointed by the Pope. Some work in Rome, assisting with the government of the Church, others work as bishops or archbishops in different dioceses throughout the world. When a Pope dies it is the task of the Cardinals to elect his successor.

Monks and nuns do not directly fit into the structure outlined above. They are members of religious communities which have grown up throughout the history of the Church – often to meet particular needs. Each Religious Order follows its own rule of life and has its own structure of authority.

WHICH IS WHICH?

What's the difference between a priest and a monk?

Monks can be priests but not all priests are monks. The majority of priests who work in parishes are not monks. That means they do not take vows, though they remain unmarried, and they do not live in communities. They are appointed by the bishop and come under his jurisdiction. They are referred to as "secular" priests.

Monks are members of religious communities and follow their own rules of life. They come under the jurisdiction of their own superior. Monks take vows of poverty, chastity and obedience. Some are ordained as priests, others (who have not been ordained) are called "brothers".

The term "monk" usually refers to members of the older Religious Orders. Communities which have been founded more recently (since the Reformation) tend to be called "Congregations" rather than "Orders", and their members are referred to as "Religious" rather than "Monks".

SEXUAL ORIENTATION

What does the Catholic Church say about gay relationships?

Everybody needs relationships and the ability to form them positively is part of being a human person. This remains true no matter what a person's sexual orientation may be. The Catholic Church recognises this truth about human beings and is concerned that no one should feel excluded from its care. However, all Christians, whatever their sexual orientation, are called to practise self-control in their relationships. And the Church does teach that the genital expression of sexual relationships is exclusive to marriage.

Are Catholic priests usually gay?

No: Catholic priests are as assorted as any group of human beings. This means that it is likely that the proportion of priests who are gay will mirror the rest of the population in their sexual orientation. Likewise, the same moral imperatives in sexual behaviour apply to them. Like everyone else, priests have to deal with their sexuality in a constructive and creative way according to God's law. This is essential whatever a person's sexual orientation. The ability to form positive relationships with both sexes is vital for every human person, including priests. Catholic priests, however, do give up the freedom to marry when they commit themselves to the service of God and people in their particular vocation.

The Church AND THE POPE

Catholics believe that the Pope is the successor of the apostle Peter. Jesus gave Peter a position of special authority and leadership among his followers when he said: "You are Peter, and on this rock I will build my church, and the powers of death shall not prevail against it. I will give you the keys of the kingdom of heaven, and whatever you bind on earth shall be bound in heaven and whatever you loose on earth shall be loosed in heaven."

At the time of Christ Rome was the centre of the known world. Tradition has it that Peter went to Rome and was martyred there. The Pope, as Bishop of Rome, is looked upon as Peter's successor. Because the Pope inherits from Peter the title of the "rock" on which the Church is built, Catholics look to the Pope as the focus of unity within the Church. He also safeguards the truth of the faith which has been handed down.

The meaning of the infallibility of the Pope is often misunderstood. It does not mean that everything the Pope says is true or that he can never make a mistake or commit sin. Infallibility means that under certain rigorous conditions the teaching of the Pope is preserved from error by the Holy Spirit.

Papal infallibility

The conditions are these:
1. The Pope must be speaking in his capacity as chief leader and shepherd of the Church.
2. He must be clearly defining a doctrine as being a truth of faith to be accepted by the whole Church.
3. The definition must be concerned with matters of faith or morals.

The number of statements by Popes which fulfil these conditions is very small. Catholics recognise that the ordinary teachings of the Pope (in sermons, speeches, encyclical letters and so on) do not fulfil these conditions and are therefore not infallible. Catholics do, nevertheless, give due respect to all the teachings of the Pope, whether infallible statements or not.

In this section we're going to introduce you to a word you'll hear quite a lot if you're married to a Catholic. We'll tell you what the word is in a minute. But first we'd like you to think about the ways people communicate with each other. Here are a few obvious ones...

THROUGH WORDS...

THROUGH TOUCH...

THROUGH GESTURE...

THROUGH SIGNS...

All these ways of communicating involve people's **senses**. Words are spoken and **heard**. A handshake is offered and **felt**. Gestures and signs are made to be **seen**. This is the way it's **got** to be. We are physical beings and we live in a physical world. So when we communicate we **must** do it in a physical way – through our senses. But very often the things we want to communicate are **not** physical. Let's take an obvious example...

Love is something real. We can experience it. We know what it is. But it's not a **physical** reality. You can't hand someone a piece of love.

So how can you communicate your love to someone? There's only one way. You must express the hidden reality called "love" in a way that the person you love can see or hear or touch. So...
You can say it with flowers...

Or send a card...

Or whisper sweet nothings...

Or give them a cuddle...

All these are physical expressions of your love. They are not the **same** as your love. But your love is conveyed **through** them. So words, gestures and physical objects like flowers or rings become **signs** of love. But they're not like ordinary signs which simply give information. . .

The signs which convey love are **special** signs. They **do** something. They carry with them a meaning, a reality, a power which can actually change someone's life...

HE LOVES ME!!

Now Catholics are very familiar with this way of communicating. They grow up with the idea that hidden realities like "love" can be communicated through signs. And they have a word for this special kind of sign. It's the word we said we would introduce you to at the beginning...

HERE IT IS, FOLKS

SACRAMENT

A sacrament is a sign through which God communicates **his** love, **his** life, **his** forgiveness to us

WHAT SORT OF SIGN IS THAT, THEN?

YEAH! WHAT SORT OF SIGN IS THAT?

Well, the first and greatest of these signs is Jesus Christ himself.

TO HAVE SEEN ME IS TO HAVE SEEN THE FATHER

Jesus makes God present to us in a way we can see, hear and touch; in a human life. Jesus embodies God's love. So he is the sign or sacrament of God.

I'VE HEARD THAT BEFORE SOMEWHERE

YES, DEAR. IN SECTION THREE

Jesus is still alive today. Through his Spirit he lives on in the community of believers – the Church. So the Church can be called a **sacrament** too because it's a **sign** of the continuing presence of Jesus in the world.

I'VE HEARD THAT BEFORE AS WELL

IN SECTION SIX, DEAR

THIS LOOKS NEW, THOUGH

Within the Church Jesus continues to communicate the Father's love, life and forgiveness to his followers.

This can happen in all kinds of ways, but Catholics believe there are sacred moments when Jesus reaches out to them in a special way. These sacred moments are the seven sacraments of the Church.

I BET THEY'RE SIGNS, TOO

YEAH! I BET THEY'RE SIGNS, TOO

Correct. The seven sacraments make use of words, gestures and material things like oil, water, bread and wine. Through these things God reaches out and touches the lives of believers.

THE SEVEN SACRAMENTS

Baptism... Confirmation... The Eucharist... Anointing of the sick... Reconciliation (Confession)... Marriage... Holy Orders.

So when Catholics receive the sacraments they believe they are coming into contact with Jesus Christ. He communicates with them, person to person, in a way that they can see, hear and touch.

A BIT SPECIAL, THEN, ARE THEY – THESE SACRAMENTS?

Very special. And they play a major part in the lives of Catholics. For through the sacraments the love, the life, the forgiveness of God is made present and real, and is **experienced** by believers. The sacraments are God's way of saying, **"Here I am. I love you."**

TOO YOUNG TO SIN

My son is preparing to celebrate the Sacrament of Reconciliation for the first time. He seems too young to sin in any serious way. What is the point of making a child anxious about such things?

The Sacrament of Reconciliation is not meant to make anyone anxious. Its purpose is just the opposite. It provides the opportunity to reflect on our failures towards God and other people, to express sorrow for those failures, and to be assured of God's forgiveness for them. We shouldn't be too hasty in assuming that young children are unaware of doing wrong and the need to say "sorry" for it. Even very young children can be deliberately mean, cruel or selfish.

Before children make their first Confession they should be able to distinguish between deliberate and accidental actions (breaking a plate may be an accident; breaking it over your sister's head is probably deliberate). They should also be able to express their faults in their own words, and they should have some understanding that their sins affect their relationship with God who is their Father.

In general children are able to fulfil these conditions between the ages of seven and eight. If a child's moral awareness develops more slowly parents can request that first Confession be postponed.

BAPTISM REFUSED

When my wife's sister took her baby to be baptised the priest refused to do it. Isn't that wrong?

If the priest refused to do it altogether and gave no explanation he certainly was wrong. But sometimes a baby is brought for baptism and the priest knows that neither of the parents is a practising Catholic and that there is no real possibility of the child being brought up in the Catholic faith. In such a situation the priest is obliged by Church law to defer the baptism, explaining to the parents his reasons for doing so. Perhaps this was the case with your sister-in-law.

Baptism is not magic. It is the sign that someone has become a member of the Church. So it doesn't make sense to baptise a child unless its parents intend bringing it up within the Catholic faith. Catholics who don't practise their faith or who have serious difficulties with their faith need to delay their baby's baptism until they can begin to rebuild a life of faith within their own family. The priest should explain this clearly to such

"In the sacraments nature participates in the process of salvation.
Bread and wine, water and light, and all the great elements of nature become the bearers of spiritual meaning and saving power."
- Paul Tillich

parents so that they understand what is required of them before their baby can be accepted for baptism.

CALL A PRIEST

My wife was anxious for the priest to call when her mother was ill. What can he do?

He can do a number of things. First, he will administer the Sacrament of the Sick. This is a special sign of God's love and care for the sick person. It consists of a series of special prayers and blessings on behalf of the patient which offer strength, encouragement and consolation. The priest will anoint the patient with holy oil as a sign of the special blessing. He will also provide an opportunity for Confession and Holy Communion so that the sick person may be consoled and untroubled by any past events which may be causing anxiety. The priest will also bless the family and offer prayers with them for the patient.

In all these ways the priest, by his presence, shows that the Christian family cares about the person who is ill. A sick person's own prayer is also of special value to the Church because such a person is so near to Christ at such a time.

EMBARRASSING OCCASION

When our first child was baptised recently, I felt very uneasy during the service. I'm not a Catholic and could not in conscience say some of the things the parents are supposed to say during the ceremony. I left my husband to say them alone. I felt very embarrassed being put in this position. Why should I have to go through it?

It is a great pity that your first child's baptism should have been marred for you by such discomfort and embarrassment. You are not expected to say anything at a baptism, or any other service, which offends your conscience. Often there is a great desire on the part of the priest and the Catholics present to ensure that a parent who is not a Catholic shouldn't feel left out. Perhaps such enthusiasm at your baby's baptism prevented them from recognising how you felt? You must always feel absolutely free to make your feelings clear on any future occasion. Don't allow yourself to be steamrollered into a situation you are unhappy about.

SIGNS OF LIFE & LOVE

Through the seven sacraments the hand of God reaches out, in sign and symbol, and touches the lives of believers at every important moment – from birth to death. Here is a brief explanation of each of these seven sacred signs.

1. Baptism is the first of the sacraments because it is the sign by which a person who has accepted Christ becomes a member of the Church. Baptism means "plunging", and till about the year 1300 the person being baptised was totally immersed in water, signifying that they shared in the death and resurrection of Christ. Today water is poured on the head only, but the meaning is the same. Water is also a sign of cleansing from sin and a sign of new life. When babies are baptised their parents and godparents make an act of faith on the child's behalf and commit themselves to bring up the child within the family of the Church.

2. Confirmation is the sacrament in which the new life which was received in baptism is strengthened and sealed. Confirmation is a sign that the Holy Spirit, whom Jesus promised to His disciples, has come upon the Christian. If someone was baptised as a baby, Confirmation enables them to make a personal act of commitment to Christ. They now make a mature act of faith and, with the help of the Holy Spirit, freely take on the responsibility of witnessing to Christ in the world. Confirmation is normally conferred by the bishop. He lays hands on those being confirmed and anoints them on the forehead with holy oil – a symbol of strengthening.

3. The Eucharist completes a person's initiation into the Christian community. Christians are not loners. They belong to a body of believers and try to live in communion with Christ and with one another. The Eucharist is the great sign of this communion. Catholics believe that when the bread and wine are consecrated during the Eucharistic celebration (the Mass) it truly becomes the Body and Blood of Jesus Christ. So when they receive Holy Communion they believe they are united in a most intimate way to the person of Jesus, and, through him, to each other.

4. Reconciliation (popularly called "Confession") is the sign of God's continuing love and forgiveness. When Christians commit themselves to Christ it does not mean that they will never again turn away from him by sin. Catholics recognise their own weakness and their continuing need of conversion. The Sacrament of Reconciliation enables them to be reconciled to God when they have fallen away from him. When sinners are truly sorry for their sins, confess them and resolve to amend their lives, they are assured of God's forgiveness through the ministry of the priest.

5. Holy Orders is the sacrament by which men are consecrated to the ordained ministry of the Church as bishops, priests or deacons. Jesus chose twelve apostles and gave them power and authority to teach and to act in his name. Catholics look upon the bishops as successors of the apostles. Through them certain powers of the ordained ministry are handed on to priests and deacons. When a priest is ordained the bishop lays hands on him to signify the handing on of Christ's power. Through this a priest is given authority to act in the person of Christ by teaching, presiding at the Eucharist and acting as a leader in the Christian community.

6. Marriage is the sacrament through which Jesus Christ is present to two people in the love they have for each other. Further, it is a sign of the love Christ has for the whole Church. When two Christians marry they bring God's grace to each other. The priest does not administer the sacrament; the man and woman administer it to each other. The priest is there as a witness only, representing the Church. The grace the couple confer on each other helps and sustains them during their life together and assures them of God's blessing on their marriage.

7. The Anointing of the Sick is the sacrament which brings spiritual comfort to members of the Church who are seriously ill and who may be in danger of death. It expresses the concern Jesus himself showed for the sick in his life on earth. By the gift of the Holy Spirit the sick person is helped to bear suffering and to fight against it. The sick person is anointed with blessed oil on the forehead and on the hands while these words are said: "Through this holy anointing may the Lord in his love and mercy help you with the grace of the Holy Spirit. Amen. May the Lord who frees you from sin save you and raise you up. Amen."

INTERCOMMUNION

I am a practising Anglican. I am marrying a Catholic in the Catholic Church. Can I receive Holy Communion at our wedding?

This sharing of communion is allowed only on very special occasions and under certain conditions. The reason why sharing communion can only be "by way of exception" is that Catholics look upon Holy Communion as the visible sign of complete unity among members of the Church. As long as there are divisions between Christians of different traditions sharing communion would be a false sign.

Catholics earnestly desire union with other Christians, and look forward to the time when we can receive the Eucharist together in complete unity of mind and heart. Until that day comes we must do everything we can to work for the unity for which Christ prayed.

Meanwhile, for your wedding, the local priest will be guided by diocesan directives. If it is not possible for you to receive Holy Communion, why not ask the priest to give you a special blessing at the time when your partner receives? The priest will be happy to do so.

People who know next to nothing about the Catholic Church do know one thing and that is that Catholics have to go to Mass on Sundays. When you're married to a Catholic your Sunday routine is inevitably going to be affected by your partner's weekly visit to Mass.

In this section we'll try to explain **why** Sunday Mass is so important to Catholics. But explaining it isn't as straightforward as it seems.

Catholics themselves have various reasons for going to Mass – some good, some not so good. Let's start with a picture...

Jesus, you're my son. Go down there and tell them to worship me properly... or else.

Right! I'll found the Catholic Church to do the job.

Peter, you're the first Pope. Hand my message on. Tell them straight.

Yes, Lord. Leave it to me and my successors.

Right priests! Make sure everyone goes to Mass on Sundays.

OK Boss

You've got to go to Mass on Sundays... or else!

A job well done.

Until fairly recently this was the sort of picture many Catholics carried round at the back of their minds. They saw the Church as a link in a chain of command between God and humankind.

This picture led some Catholics to go to Mass on Sundays largely out of a sense of obligation and fear of God's wrath. Today most Catholics would agree that the above picture is grossly misleading. It's misleading for three reasons:

> 1. It makes God out to be a tyrant who is out to get you unless you kowtow to him.
>
> 2. It makes Jesus out to be God's henchman who came to tell us what to do.
>
> 3. It makes the Church out to be an organisation set up by Jesus to make sure we do it.

If you've followed the earlier sections of this book you'll realise that none of these three statements is true. And none of them accurately represents the belief of Catholics today.

SEE ESPECIALLY SECTIONS TWO, THREE AND SIX

Nowadays the majority of Catholics have much more mature reasons for going to Mass than fear of God's anger. But that old picture does still have **some** influence and occasionally you **will** come across Catholics who go to Mass just to "keep their slate clean"...

WELL THAT'S **ME** IN THE CLEAR FOR ANOTHER WEEK

You'll also come across Catholics who go to Mass out of a sense of fear and foreboding. They think something terrible will happen to them during the week if they miss Mass on Sunday.

I'LL GET YOU BAGLEY

Much more frequently you'll come across Catholics who go to Mass because it would be awkward not to go. This is particularly true of some teenagers who go because the rest of the family goes, but given the choice they'd rather stay in bed.

COME ON!

But the majority of Catholics go to Mass on Sunday because they believe it is central to their lives as Christians. So let's look at what Catholics believe is happening when they go to Mass.

The first thing to say is that Catholics don't think of the Mass as a church service which they attend. The Mass is an **action**. It is something Catholics **do** together. They're not spectators **at it**; they're deeply involved **in it**.

At Mass they re-enact what Jesus did at the supper he had with his disciples on the night before he was crucified.

Here's how the Gospel of Luke describes it:

He took bread, and when he had given thanks he broke it and gave it to them, saying, "This is my body which is given for you. Do this in remembrance of me." And likewise the cup after supper, saying, "This cup which is poured out for you is the new covenant in my blood…"

The words of Jesus "Do this in remembrance of me" have been obeyed without interruption for nearly 2,000 years. Every time Catholics gather for Mass they know they are there to do what Jesus did. And they believe that in that action Jesus, who died on the cross and was raised to life three days later, is made present for them.

The Mass is a sacred action which has a depth of meaning impossible to put into words. That's one reason why Catholics never tire of the Mass. As they go to Mass over the weeks and months and years they enter more deeply into its mystery and get a bit more insight into its significance and its meaning for their own lives.

So if you asked a number of Catholics what the Mass means to them you'd probably get a lot of **different** answers. Here are some of the things they might say…

The Mass teaches you to accept God's gifts gratefully. You can never be worthy of them.

Sometimes it's boring or there's a baby screaming, and it's hard to feel anything but deep down you know it's very special.

The Mass isn't for **me**, it's for **us**. We're a community of believers and the Mass holds us together.

If I didn't go to Mass I'd forget about God altogether. It keeps me in touch

The Mass brings me into contact with the sacrifice of Christ on the Cross

Communion is the most important part for me. It's such a privilege to receive the Body of Christ

At Mass I leave all my worries behind and focus on what's really important in my life

It's a weekly reminder that there's more to life than increasing your standard of living

I bring my worries with me and offer them to God

Shluggle duggle

You touch holy things at Mass

Sunday was the day Jesus rose from the dead. We come together to celebrate that

For me the Mass is **worship**. I'm not the centre of the universe, **God is**. At Mass I acknowledge that

There's a lot more we could say about the Mass, but we hope we've said enough to show that for Catholics the Mass isn't a weekly chore. It's something very precious to them. That's why it plays such a central part in their lives.

SOME THINGS YOU SEE AT MASS

1. Scripture readings:
usually three passages from the scriptures are read at Mass.

2. Homily:
after the scripture readings the priest preaches a sermon in which he draws out the meaning of the scripture readings.

3. Offertory procession:
members of the congregation bring the bread and wine to the altar.

TWO ALTERNATIVES

Why can't Catholics pray at home instead of going to Mass?

Catholics can and do pray at home. They don't do it as a substitute for going to Mass because it is a different form of prayer and has a different purpose. It's not simply a question of choosing one of two alternatives. Christians are essentially a group of people who believe in Jesus Christ and try to follow his way. They are a community of believers. If the members of any family or community never have any contact with one another they soon cease to be united and disintegrate into isolation.

Catholics attend Mass because it is the culmination of their lives as Christians. In the Mass they are united to one another and to Christ in a unique and personal way. But they pray at home as well.

SUNDAY EXCUSE

My Catholic husband uses Sunday Mass as an excuse not to visit my family. Surely the Church shouldn't be used to cause trouble in families?

You are right, the Church shouldn't be used to cause trouble. In fact the opposite is the truth: Christianity should be the means of healing over differences and divisions. Your husband has an obligation to attend Sunday Mass, but he also has an equally serious obligation to share his life with you and to work towards unity and harmony within your marriage. He must work out, with your

help and support, how he may best fulfil **all** his obligations. If he doesn't like your family and is seeking an excuse not to see them he is very wrong to use the Church as the reason. In doing so he is betraying the principles of his faith.

SELF-CONSCIOUS

When I go to Mass with my husband I feel left out and self-conscious because I am unfamiliar with the prayers. I am also uneasy in case I'll be expected to do something I'm not ready for. I feel everyone's staring at me. Wouldn't it be better if I didn't go at all?

The feeling of being stared at in unfamiliar surroundings is understandable. But be assured that people are **not** staring at you. Most Catholics are not the least bit concerned about what anyone else is doing during Mass – and many of them have their own idiosyncrasies! Some Catholics do not join in the prayers, for example, so you won't be alone if you remain silent.

Ask your husband to show you the book or leaflet you need to follow the Mass and also where the responses are indicated. Once you get used to the form the Mass takes you will feel much more relaxed.

There are a few days during the year when there are special ceremonies: Maundy Thursday and Good Friday, for example. If you attend these ask your husband to run through the ceremony with you beforehand so that you'll know what to expect.

INSENSITIVE PRIESTS

I've been to Mass with my husband on a number of occasions and it never seems to occur to the priest that there might be people in the congregation who are not Catholics. Why are they so insensitive?

Most Catholic priests would be delighted to know that people who are not Catholics are present in their congregation, especially if they are the husband or wife of a parishioner. You are probably right when you say, "It doesn't occur to them." It would undoubtedly help if you made yourself known to the parish priest, or perhaps your husband could introduce you.

FEAST DAYS

I can understand my wife going to Mass on Sundays but why does she have to go during the week as well if some special "feast day" crops up?

The days you refer to are called "holy-days of obligation". These are days of special solemnity in the Church's calendar which Catholics observe by going to Mass – rather in the same way that families celebrate birthdays or anniversaries.

DILEMMA

Am I expected to take the children to Mass on Sunday if my wife is ill? No, you are not expected to take them. If they are old enough they can take themselves, if they are too young to do that then there is no obligation for them

4. Elevation:
after the consecration the priest lifts the host and then the chalice so that they may be venerated by the people.

5. Sign of peace:
the people express their union with one another by exchanging a greeting – usually a handshake.

6. Holy Communion:
is distributed to all who wish to receive.

to attend Sunday Mass. If the problem is one of distance or transport then the decision is yours. Certainly, you have no obligation in this matter. It would simply be a question of whether you wished to take them on behalf of your wife.

BORING MASS

I have been to Mass a few times with my wife and two young children and it has always been boring. Why?

In some parishes, sadly, the Mass nearly always is boring – even for Catholics. These are usually parishes where not very much care seems to be taken over the Mass by priest or people. Half-hearted singing, inaudible readers and dull, uninspiring sermons are some of the symptoms. Obviously it should not be like that. The Mass is a celebration of Christ's presence among us. In the Mass Catholics believe they come into contact with Christ and that their prayers are united to his. This happens whether the ceremonies are "performed" well or not. Nevertheless, priest and people have a responsibility to see that the meaning of the Mass is conveyed in the way it is celebrated.

In places where the Mass is celebrated in a lifeless and off-hand manner, some Catholics "shop around" for another parish where the Mass is celebrated with care, dignity and beauty. "Shopping around" is not ideal because everyone should worship with their own parish community. But it's sometimes very understandable – especially for families with young children.

LEFT OUT

Must my wife take our son to Mass every Sunday? I feel left out and he is beginning to ask: "Why doesn't Daddy come to Mass?"

If your son has made his First Holy Communion your wife is expected to ensure that he practises his faith and attends Mass regularly. But it is important that she does not use your son to bring pressure on you to alter your views or to "blackmail" you into attending Mass.

You and your wife should explain to your son, as simply as you can, that you do not share the same faith. The mutual respect you show to each other in this matter will help him to understand your differences of belief.

When your son is old enough he will be able to decide whether to go to Mass with your wife, or on his own, or with his friends.

FROM CHURCH TO PUB

Many Catholics go to Mass every Sunday and then straight across to the pub. Doesn't that indicate that the Mass doesn't mean a lot to them?

No. It could mean the opposite. Perhaps they so enjoyed meeting their friends at Mass that they didn't want to part company straight away! There's nothing wrong with social contact after a religious service: coffee and biscuits in the hall, a glass of sherry at a friend's house, or a pint at the pub or club. None of these lessens the sincerity of the religious service.

Christ's message is all about loving and caring for one another and the value of friendship. Of course if we stay too long at such a gathering or neglect our families, causing disharmony at home as a result, then we **do** need to question our behaviour. But that would apply to attending the religious service too.

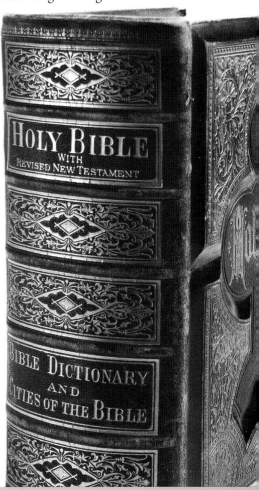

The main thing to realise about the Catholic Church's attitude to marriage is that it's the same as everybody else's. Everybody loves a good wedding. Especially aunts.

Everybody likes to see a happy couple who love each other enough to want to spend the rest of their lives together. Their love, hope and trust strike deep chords in people's hearts.

At a wedding everyone recognises that two people have found something of immense value. They've been taken out of their loneliness and have discovered, in their love for each other, a new sense of meaning and purpose in their lives.

This is so important to them that they want to make it permanent and they want to make it public.

So in the presence of their family and friends they pledge their undying love.

The Catholic Church is entirely in agreement with all of this. Like nearly everybody else the Catholic Church thinks marriage is wonderful.

True enough. But as Christianity developed, married Christians began to realise that their love for each other was the same love that was at the heart of their Christian faith.

So for Christians marriage took on a much deeper meaning. They began to realise that the bond of love between a married couple not only brought them closer to each other, but also brought them closer to Christ.

Christians began to look upon marriage not only as a social institution but as a way to holiness.

And that's not all. The love married people showed each other didn't only have an effect on the couple themselves. It was also a **sign** for the whole Church.

SEE HOW THEY LOVE EACH OTHER

THEY'RE SO CARING AND GENTLE

AND TOLERANT AND FORGIVING

THE LOVE OF CHRIST MUST BE A BIT LIKE THAT

So marriage came to be recognised as a SACRAMENT – one of those seven signs by which the love of Christ is made visible in the world.

Now all this may sound a little bit unrealistic. Most people would say that marriage just isn't like that.

MY TEACHER SAYS MARRIED PEOPLE MAKE CHRIST PRESENT TO EACH OTHER

How, then, do married people become a sign of Christ's love for each other and the people round them?

Chiefly by discovering what love is and what it means. Marriage has been called a school of love. And most people have a lot to learn.

When the honeymoon's over and the romance has worn off, all married couples have to discover what true love means. Over the weeks and months and years of their relationship there are numerous opportunities for learning to accept, to be tolerant, to forgive.

I'm sorry, dear. I put my foot on the accelerator instead of the brake and ran the new car into the greenhouse. Oh...and my mother's coming to stay for a fortnight...

ARGH!

Hello, dear. I'm bringing some of the lads home from the darts team. Can you rustle up some supper for them – only five of us. And I'll need a clean shirt for tomorrow...

ARGH!

It's by discovering what love really means and being faithful to it that married Christians come closer to Christ themselves and show something of Christ's love to other Christians.

That's one reason why the Catholic Church insists that marriage is for life. It's only in the life-long fidelity of married love that the total faithfulness of Christ's love can be truly symbolised.

TILL DEATH DO US PART

It should be obvious by now that the Catholic concept of marriage involves much more than simply holding the wedding in church. What makes a marriage Christian isn't a church blessing added on to a legal contract. Christian marriage is a personal relationship of life-giving love in which two people make the love of Christ present to each other and become a sign of the love of Christ to those around them.

This is a high ideal, a sacred ideal. And it's because of this that the Church places so much emphasis on preparation for marriage. The Church wants couples to understand what they're taking on. As far as the Church is concerned a wedding isn't a happy ending to a love story. It's a happy beginning to a life-long relationship of love in Christ.

> **"Success in marriage is more than finding the right person: it is a matter of being the right person."**
> — Rabbi B R Brickner

CHURCH WEDDING

Why do Catholics have to get married in church?

First, there's a purely practical reason. It is a way of recording when and where Catholics marry. Parish records serve a useful purpose in both civil and Church matters.

But a much more important reason is that marriage, in the eyes of Catholics, is a sacrament – one of those seven sacred signs through which God communicates his love to us. When Catholics marry they believe that God ratifies their union. The love of the couple for each other is a sign of God's love for each of them. This is expressed during the wedding ceremony in the words: "What God has joined together, let no man put asunder."

The union of the couple themselves is also a sign – a continuous sign of Christ's love for the Church. As St Paul put it: "Husbands should love their wives just as Christ loved the Church and sacrificed himself for her..."

So when Catholics marry they do not look upon it simply as a contract which a man and a woman make between themselves. They see it as something in which God is deeply involved and which also involves the whole Christian community. That is why the wedding takes place in church.

HIGH IDEAL

The Catholic concept of marriage and family life is very demanding and full of high ideals. I'm afraid I just don't feel able to live up to it. What is the minimum I am expected to do?

The fact that you are marrying a Catholic does not mean that you are expected to do anything more than might be expected in any marriage. In every marriage both partners have to be sensitive to each other's feelings and opinions. In every marriage there has to be room for adjustment and understanding.

Every marriage has its ups and downs, too. So you shouldn't imagine that you have to live up to an impossibly high ideal in which, for example, there are no rows and no problems. Just because you are married to a Catholic it doesn't mean that a good shouting match is somehow a sign of failure. It is precisely by working through problems and difficulties that the ideal of Christian marriage and family life gradually becomes a reality.

ANGLICAN CEREMONY

I am a practising Anglican and my fiancée is a Catholic. I am keen that the marriage should take place in my own church. Is this allowed?

Yes, in certain circumstances the Church can dispense a Catholic from the normal rule for a Catholic marriage. Your fiancée should discuss this question with her parish priest and explain the reason why she would like to marry in the Anglican church. Such requests to be married in another's church are usually considered sympathetically these days.

The reason why a dispensation is required is that the normal rule for a Catholic marriage is that the marriage vows are exchanged before a bishop, priest or deacon and two witnesses. The Church is concerned that the Catholic preparing for marriage should see a priest and receive all the help which the Church can offer. And also, because marriage between two Christians is a sacrament, the Church wishes to join her prayers with those of the couple.

MIXED MARRIAGES

Does the Catholic Church disapprove of mixed marriages?

In the past the Church frowned on mixed marriages, principally because they were seen as a threat to the faith of the Catholic and his or her children. Today, the Church recognises the value of the faith and love, and the opportunities for growth and understanding between such couples.

There can be challenges in such marriages: problems of principle and conscience which require a lot of heart-searching and trusting love if hurt and misunderstanding are to be avoided. Catholics undertake to do all in their power to baptise and bring up their children in the Catholic faith and to protect their own faith. A partner who is not a Catholic doesn't have to make any promises but must be aware of the Catholic's undertaking. The beliefs and rights of that partner must also be respected by the Catholic. At the wedding ministers of both faiths may participate, and, for serious reasons, a Catholic entering a mixed marriage may marry in a church of another denomination. A special dispensation is needed for this. Successive Popes have spoken on the value of signs of unity between Christians. A good mixed marriage is a living sign of the unity that is possible between those of goodwill.

PUSHED AROUND

I am marrying a Catholic and we have been to some talks. It seems I have to do what the Church wants. They don't seem concerned about my wishes.

It's a pity if this is the impression you have been given for it is an utterly false one. One of the aims of such talks is to emphasise the equal importance and value of **both** partners in the marriage. The Church insists that each person's feelings, expectations and loyalties should be recognised and respected. Marriage preparation aims to ensure

When a petition for nullity is made to the Church, the petition is investigated by one of the Church's marriage tribunals – a panel of judges set up for this purpose. If, when they have weighed all the evidence, they find that the grounds for annulment have been proved they can pronounce the marriage null and void. In other words, they declare that there was never a true marriage in the first place.

This is where nullity differs from divorce. Divorce means that a true and valid marriage is dissolved (and Catholics believe no one has the power to do that). But to pronounce a marriage null is to recognise that there was never a true marriage.

Annulment is possible because certain conditions are necessary before a valid marriage can take place. The partners must give their consent **freely**, they must have the **intention** of marrying and they must be **capable** of marrying. If any of these conditions was absent at the time of the wedding then the marriage can be declared null.

The fact that a marriage has broken down is not, by itself, sufficient proof that there never was a marriage. Many valid marriages break down through human weakness or culpability of one or both partners. The Church has no power to dissolve a truly constituted marriage.

A decree of nullity in no way affects the legitimacy of any children.

that a couple really have explored and considered every aspect of marriage and what it will mean to them.

Your partner has an obligation to make a positive attempt to understand and respect your point of view and principles. And you are expected to do likewise for your partner. Do not be shy of stating your wishes and ideas; they are a valuable part of what makes you the kind of person you are, and your Catholic partner needs to know and understand this for your future happiness together.

KEY POINTS
What points should I consider before marrying a Catholic?

Marriage is the most important decision you'll make in your life. So the main points you should consider are the ones **everybody** should consider when they're thinking of getting married – whether to a Catholic or not.

Ask yourself these questions:

● Can I spend the rest of my life with my prospective partner? Am I capable of sustaining this relationship day in and day out for a lifetime?

● Is my partner capable of this sort of relationship with me?

● Can I be relied on to love and cherish my partner in good times and bad, in sickness and in health?

● Can I rely on my partner to do the same for me?

● Does my partner know me sufficiently well (my bad points as well as good) to make a life-long commitment to me?

● Do I know my partner well enough to do the same?

● Am I getting married of my own free will? Am I sure there's no pressure on me from any source at all?

If you cannot honestly answer "yes" to all these questions, think again. A broken engagement is upsetting, but a broken marriage is a disaster.

If you are marrying a Catholic you should also ask yourself whether you have any strong objections to your children being brought up as Catholics. If you have, please talk this over very carefully with your partner **before** you get married. Failure to do so could lead to serious problems later on.

Finally, remember that Catholics put great emphasis on the **permanence** of marriage. On your wedding day you'll make a solemn vow "to have and to hold...till death do us part". If you have any doubts about your own or your partner's ability to keep that vow, or if you have any doubts about your sincerity in making it, don't get married.

PREPARING FOR MARRIAGE
Why do my fiancée and I have to attend marriage preparation classes?

The reason is simple. Catholics believe marriage is for life. This is a serious commitment and a demanding one. When two people are deeply in love it is all too easy to gloss over difficult or controversial issues, only to have them arise after the wedding as serious problems.

The priest has to ensure that to the best of his knowledge any couple who marry within the Church are mature, able to fulfil the solemn vows they make, and understand the nature of their undertaking. It would be most unfair if the Church allowed people to marry

without any preparation and then expected them to live up to a standard which they did not realise they were committing themselves to.

CATHOLICS AND DIVORCE
How is it that some Catholics get a divorce?

When their marriage breaks down some Catholics get a **civil** divorce in order to protect their property, inheritance or security. Catholics believe a marriage between Christians can never be dissolved. So although for legal reasons a Catholic may get a civil divorce, the Church still considers them to be married and they cannot remarry in the Church. Such people may, however, continue to receive Holy Communion and still remain full members of the Church.

MARRIAGE ANNULMENT
Is nullity a Catholic divorce?

No. It is official Church recognition that the marriage was not a true marriage in the first place. This can only be if, on examination, it is found that one or several of the requirements of a vaild marriage were not present. This sometimes involves a long procedure and requires witnesses and evidence to support any claim of invalidity. It cannot be bought or arranged.

◆ ◆ ◆

How's this for a picture of the Catholic Church's attitude to sex?

THIS WAY

Many people would say it's a very accurate picture – including many Catholics.

SURE WOULD

We must be honest and admit that the Catholic Church's teaching on sex has often been presented in a negative and pessimistic way. For centuries it was a commonly held view that the primary and dominant purpose of sex was the procreation of children. So much emphasis was placed on this that the purely pleasurable aspects of sex were viewed with suspicion. This negative and sometimes fearful attitude to sex continued into the 20th century

and left its mark on many Catholics. Here's a quotation from an interview with a Catholic woman in her forties:

"It took me a very long time to develop an honest sexual relationship with my husband… Most of it was because of my old-fashioned Catholic upbringing. I wouldn't allow love-play or anything like that – it felt very sinful. And consequently love-making was a tremendous disappointment."

Some married Catholics are still uneasy about their sex lives, but the picture is changing. There has always been a strand in the Church's teaching which recognises that the sexual union

between a man and a woman has a much deeper meaning than a purely biological one. In the past this was often underplayed but in more recent times it has gradually come to the fore. As a result a much more positive view of human sexuality has emerged in the Catholic Church.

ABOUT TIME TOO

HEAR, HEAR!

Official Church pronouncements don't make easy reading but the following short quotation does give some indication of the Church's present attitude towards sex.

IT'S FROM THE SECOND VATICAN COUNCIL

Married love is uniquely expressed and perfected in the exercise of the **acts proper to marriage.** Hence the acts in marriage by which the intimate and chaste union of the spouses takes place are **noble** and **honourable**; the truly human performance of these acts fosters the **self-giving** they signify and enriches the spouses in **joy** and **gratitude**.

THAT MEANS SEX FOLKS

That may sound a bit highfalutin, but it does at least show that the Church's attitude to sex is no longer based on suspicion. The Church does recognise that **sex is a good thing**.

IF THEY'D ASKED US, WE COULD'VE TOLD THEM THAT

Actually, one encouraging sign is that the Church has begun to listen to married couples and to take their experiences into account.

Here are two more extracts from interviews with Catholic married women. These express something of the depth and richness of a fulfilled sexual relationship.

> "I feel that a happy sexual relationship is very important in a marriage. I find that an awful lot of the hurts of a normal aggravating week are healed when we make love. I feel wanted, cared about and loved – and a lot of other problems don't seem to matter so much."

> "I don't think you realise when you're young how important sex is in a marriage. For myself it wasn't for years that I was able to realise that the joining of two bodies to become one was a very spiritual, soul-satisfying experience. It's only when it's part of the true unity of the couple… that it becomes the beautiful, special act that it is… in which both partners are enriched and given new vitality to their love."

It's interesting to compare these two quotations with the extract from the official Church document we quoted earlier. All three have a very **high** view of sex.

Of its nature sex is a **physical** act, but its **meaning** goes much deeper. It has the power to heal, to soothe, to reassure.

Through their sexual union a couple come to a deeper knowledge of each other – and this promotes growth, trust and security. Through sex they can express their joy and gratitude to each other.

Sex is a body-language – a language which has the power to communicate the deepest thoughts, feelings, and needs of the partners.

In other words, sex builds up, deepens and cements the **relationship** between two people.

And that's one reason why the Catholic Church says that sex can only find full and authentic expression within the permanent commitment of marriage.

Sex outside marriage is likely to be impoverished. First because the two people involved can't be sure they **mean** the same thing:

And second because outside marriage sex doesn't have the chance to express its full potential:

The Catholic Church recognises the power, the beauty, the rich potentiality of the sexual act. It's because of the **high** value it places on sex that the Church maintains that sex and marriage must go together.

In other words, making love should **mean** making love. By giving themselves to each other sexually a couple are increasing their love for each other and encouraging it to **grow**. It's only within a secure, stable and permanent relationship that this has a chance to happen.

STOP MEDDLING

I don't see what sex and marriage have got to do with Christianity. Why doesn't the Church stick to praying and stop meddling in people's personal affairs?

The teaching of Jesus Christ is not concerned with "religion" in a closed and narrow sense. His teaching ranges over the whole of human experience as is summed up in his own words: "I have come that they may have life and have it to the full."

Christians believe that Jesus came to show us how to be fully human and fully alive. So there are no areas of our lives which are barred to his influence.

Sex and marriage are central to the lives of most people. It is within a loving relationship that the majority of human beings seek fulfilment and growth in human maturity. It would be very surprising if Christianity had nothing at all to say about such a relationship.

Christian faith isn't just for church on Sundays. It's concerned with the whole of life – especially those aspects of it that are most important to us.

TOO MANY CHILDREN

Why is the Catholic Church so opposed to family planning? Surely it's unreasonable to expect a couple to have as many children as they can?

The Catholic Church is not opposed to family planning. In fact, the Church encourages married couples to plan their families responsibly. Confusion about the Church's teaching on this subject arises because terms like "family planning", "birth control" and "contraception" are often used as though they all mean the same thing.

The Catholic Church **is** opposed to artificial methods of contraception like the pill, the cap, the sheath etc. But it is not opposed to the principle of family planning. Married couples **should** make a reasonable decision about the number of children they have and how they should be spaced. In doing so they should take into account things like their financial and housing situation, and their own readiness and ability to care for a child. When a couple are first married they may decide not to have a child immediately – and there can be very good reasons for this. They may want time to grow closer

"Sex is one of the most powerful means of life-giving. On a few occasions it is used deliberately to give a new life and on every occasion acts as a renewal of the life of the couple and through them of the family." — Jack Dominian

together as a couple before taking on the responsibility of bringing a child into the world. Or they may want to establish their home first.

Provided the decision to postpone or space your family is taken for sound reasons (and is not based on purely selfish motives) the Church most certainly approves.

CONTRACEPTION
Why does the Catholic Church forbid the use of the pill and other contraceptives? I don't see any difference between using the pill and using natural methods of family planning. The aim in both cases is exactly the same.

Let's start at the beginning: why does the Catholic Church forbid the use of the pill?

If you ask what sexual intercourse is **for**, it's fairly obvious that it has **two** functions. The first is to express and bring about the loving union of a man and a woman. Every time they make love they strengthen and deepen their relationship with each other. The second function of sexual intercourse is the procreation of children. By expressing their own love, a couple can co-operate with the creative action of God, making it possible to bring new life into the world.

The Catholic Church holds that these two functions of sexual intercourse cannot be separated. They are built into the sexual act rather in the same way that enjoyment of food on the one hand, and its necessity for nourishing the body on the other, are **both** built into the act of eating. In other words, **both** the functions of sexual intercourse are part of God's design and we cannot separate them on our own initiative. This is because **God** is the ultimate source of life, not us. So when people take steps to separate the two functions of sexual intercourse to ensure that the possibility of procreation is removed, they are claiming a domination over life which they do not possess. This, briefly, is why the Church forbids the use of contraceptives.

But there is no opposition to God's design when couples restrict their love-making to the infertile days in the woman's cycle. When they do that they are simply making use of a facility which is provided by nature itself (or, in Christian terms, by God himself). The pill and other contraceptives, on the other hand, are designed to obstruct the natural processes of procreation at times when the woman **is** fertile.

NATURAL METHODS
Does the Catholic Church recommend natural methods of birth control because they're NOT very reliable?

The Church is not a family planning agency; it doesn't "recommend" anything! The Church's concern is with the **morality** of birth regulation. (The moral arguments for the Church's ban on artificial methods of birth control are outlined in the answer to the previous question.) It should be noted that the use of natural methods may also be immoral if adopted for purely selfish motives. For example, if a couple wanted to avoid having children simply so that they could live in ease and comfort themselves with no ties, they would – in the Church's view – be acting immorally: even if they were using natural methods of birth control.

So the reliability or otherwise of natural methods does not come into it. For the Church the question is essentially a **moral** one.

However, since your question implies a certain cynicism about the reliability of natural methods, it might be worth pointing out that there have been considerable advances in this area in recent years. When natural methods are properly taught and properly used their success rate is high. People who are not Catholics are becoming more and more attracted to them because they do not have the disadvantages of some artificial methods – the possibility of side-effects with the pill, for example.

CATHOLICS AND THE PILL
Someone told me recently that you can't be a Catholic if you are on the pill. Is that true?

No, it is not. Some people, like your informant, think that because the Church teaches that contraception is wrong, Catholics who use artificial methods of birth control put themselves outside the Church. This is to misunderstand the nature of the Church. We have pointed out several times in this book that the Church is not a sort of club for virtuous or religious people. It is made up of ordinary people who are trying to be friends and followers of Jesus Christ but who often fail in all sorts of ways to live up to their Christian ideals. Within the Church they know the forgiveness of Christ is always available to them and that, whatever their sins, they can always make a fresh start. The Church, like Christ himself, is extremely tolerant of sinners.

The Church also understands the pressures people may have to contend with in their lives, and therefore takes into account not only what people **do** but also the circumstances which surround what they do. In other words, the Church recognises that it is possible for someone to do something which, objectively speaking, is wrong but – because of the circumstances – the individual who performs the wrong action may not be personally culpable.

This principle can be applied in the case of contraception. While no Catholic may reject any part of the Church's teaching, or say that it does not apply in his or her case, there may well be circumstances in which a Catholic couple may conscientiously decide for unselfish reasons that they cannot further increase their family and that the only option open to them is to practise contraception. In their circumstances this decision could be defensible.

No one has the right to judge that couples who have made such a decision are no longer Catholics or that they are disloyal or second-class Catholics. This is especially so when the full intimate circumstances of a couple are not known. God alone is the judge of consciences.

KEEPING IT SECRET
I'm soon to be married to a man who is a Catholic, though I have no religious beliefs myself. I want children but not right away. Supposing I take the pill without telling him. Wouldn't this be the simplest solution for both of us?

Not a good idea. Your marriage would be starting completely on the wrong foot if you were deceiving him about something so central to your relationship. The decision about when to have children is an important one for both of you and it should be arrived at by mutual agreement. The method of family planning you choose should also be something you are **both** happy with. Marriage is a partnership, so it's important to talk this over together and try to reach a solution acceptable to both of you.

We'd like to start this section by asking you a question. What do you want most for your children? Of course, different people will answer that in different ways...

SHE'S GOING TO BE A CELEBRITY

AND HE'S A FUTURE CHARTERED ACCOUNTANT

So let's narrow it down a bit and imagine a fairy godmother making you this offer...

Two magic jars I offer you
Containing gifts so rare.
Three gifts are yours to give a child,
Three only can I spare.
Just one condition I lay down
Before you come to choose:
All three must be
from the same jar –
Now what have you got to lose?

WHO WROTE HER SCRIPT?

Now, here are the jars. Which three gifts would you choose for a child? Remember, all three must be from the same jar.

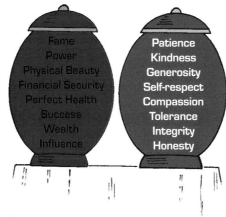

Fame	Patience
Power	Kindness
Physical Beauty	Generosity
Financial Security	Self-respect
Perfect Health	Compassion
Success	Tolerance
Wealth	Integrity
Influence	Honesty

There are several considerations that parents might take into account in trying to reach a decision.

Mr and Mrs A might look at it like this...

WE'VE CHOSEN FROM THE RED JAR PERFECT HEALTH, WEALTH AND INFLUENCE

WE WANT OUR SON TO GO INTO POLITICS AND THEY'RE THE THREE THINGS WE THINK HE'LL NEED MOST

Mr and Mrs B might look at it like this...

WE'VE CHOSEN FROM THE BLUE JAR BECAUSE THE CONTENTS ARE MORE LIKELY TO BRING A PERSON HAPPINESS

THAN ANYTHING IN THE RED JAR

SO WE'VE CHOSEN KINDNESS, SELF-RESPECT AND INTEGRITY

Mr and Mrs C might look at it like this...

WE'VE CHOSEN FROM THE RED JAR - PHYSICAL BEAUTY, FINANCIAL SECURITY, AND PERFECT HEALTH

HERE'S WHY: WE DON'T THINK YOU **NEED** A FAIRY GOD-MOTHER TO PROVIDE THE THINGS IN THE BLUE JAR. IT'S OUR JOB AS PARENTS TO GIVE THESE GIFTS TO OUR CHILDREN

BUT THE THINGS IN THE RED JAR ARE OUTSIDE ANYONE'S CONTROL, SO WE MIGHT AS WELL TAKE ADVANTAGE OF THE FAIRY GOD-MOTHER

Which couple would you go along with? Whatever your answer, Mr and Mrs C have obviously made a good point. For most of us, the contents of the red jar are outside anyone's control, but the contents of the blue jar are not. Parents, by their love, care, influence and example, can lay the foundations which will encourage a child to develop the sort of gifts contained in the blue jar.

ALL RIGHT. I KNOW WHEN I'M NOT WANTED

That's why the Catholic Church lays so much emphasis on the importance of family life. A happy and stable family provides the kind of atmosphere in which a child learns to relate to

others: to care, to share, to love, to forgive.

In other words, the really important things in a child's life don't happen in school or in church. They happen in the home. It's in the home that children learn that they're loved and accepted. And this forms the basis of their image of themselves, their relationships with other people and their relationship with God.

So parents are their children's first and most important teachers.

In this role they're never off duty. Everything they do and say rubs off on their children and has an influence – for good or bad.

TELL YOUR MOTHER I'M OFF TO THE PUB AND I'LL BE BACK VERY LATE

TELL YOUR FATHER NOT TO BOTHER COMING BACK

The way they speak to each other, the way they treat each other, the way they cope with disagreements, the way they show tolerance and forgiveness are all vitally important.

There's a place for more formal teaching, too, especially religious teaching. Catholics believe it's important for children to establish a loving relationship with God at an early age. This can be done very simply by building on children's natural appreciation of the world around them.

It's only a short step from this to making up simple prayers which express wonder or thanksgiving or praise. In Catholic families, prayers like these are often said with young children at bedtime. If both parents join in it can become a very special time in a child's day.

WE SAY 'THANK YOU' TO GOD OUR FATHER FOR THE LOVELY SUNSHINE TODAY...

Catholic children usually celebrate the Sacrament of Reconciliation and make their First Holy Communion round about the age of seven, and they are confirmed between the ages of about eleven and fourteen. Parents are encouraged to take an active part in the preparation of the sacraments. So you may be asked to attend some talks to explain what's involved.

These sacraments are a landmark in a child's religious development and Catholic parents are usually eager to do everything they can to prepare for them and make them

memorable occasions. Your partner will appreciate your support and co-operation at these special times.

The main Christian festivals also have a special place in Catholic family life. Catholics are all in favour of merry-making and they welcome a bank holiday as much as anyone else. But festivals like Christmas and Easter have a much deeper significance for them. The reason for celebrating is a religious one and they like to keep that uppermost in their minds. Although you may not wish to go to Mass with your family every Sunday, you might like to think about going with them on these special festivals. It would mean a lot to your partner.

THE FIRST NOWELL...

In today's world it's not easy to bring up a family within a Christian framework. The values of a consumer society are so often opposed to the values of Jesus Christ. At times you may feel under pressure because you can't keep up the standard of living you would like, or give your children all the things they want. But you and your partner have a much greater gift to give: the love and security of a happy home.

"God could not be everywhere, so he made mothers."
— Jewish proverb

"It is easier for a father to have children than for children to have a real father."
— Pope John XXIII

BRINGING UP CHILDREN

What part am I expected to play in bringing up our children as Catholics?

The obligations in this matter are on your Catholic partner, not on you. But your partner will appreciate any interest you show or moral support you feel able to give in the religious education of your children. It is important, too, that you are willing to explain to your children your beliefs and ideas about religion. In this way they will learn to be understanding and tolerant of differing views – an important part of any Christian education.

UNFAIR TREATMENT

When you're married to a Catholic your home life seems to revolve round Catholic principles. I seem to have to give in to them all along the line. Is that fair?

If that's how you are made to feel it is certainly not at all fair. Catholics are supposed to be trying to live sincerely as Christians. And being a Christian does not mean putting burdens on other people's shoulders or ignoring their opinions and beliefs. A Catholic whose partner is not a Catholic needs to be particularly sensitive about this.

Your ideas and beliefs should not be ignored and you should make this clear to your partner. Try to discuss your differences of opinion openly so that your partner understands your point of view.

PRE-NATAL SCREENING

I'm expecting our first child and have been offered pre-natal screening tests. If they show that the baby is disabled I would want an abortion. My husband is a Catholic. Would he object to this?

Many of the screening tests offered to expectant mothers are extremely useful in checking the progress of the pregnancy and providing early warning of any trouble, which may then be rectified. Some of them also predict whether the baby is likely to be disabled. Unfortunately, experience has shown that such predictions are by no means completely reliable and instances have been reported where a baby has been aborted and then found to be perfectly normal. Other babies have been born disabled or with learning difficulties although tests revealed no abnormality. The first lesson, then, is that these tests are not 100% accurate. You could destroy a perfectly normal baby.

The Catholic Church is opposed to abortion, for any reason, because it is the deliberate killing of another human being. The fact that the baby is very small does not alter that.

The birth of a baby with some disability is a traumatic experience and the Catholic Church is very insistent that proper care and support be provided for all disabled people and their families. There is ample evidence that disabled people and those with severe learning difficulties, given the appropriate help, can live just as fulfilled and enriching lives as anyone else.

Many women refuse screening tests which may result in offers of an abortion. In this way they avoid the slight risk involved in having these tests and they also avoid several months of sometimes needless anxiety which can cloud their pregnancy.

GODPARENTS
My family are not Catholics but I would very much like my sister to be godmother to our baby son. Is this allowed?

Godparents go back to the days when most adult converts to the Christian faith had no Christian parents. They spoke up for the baptised person and, if necessary, helped him or her to grow in the faith. But most parents choose two. When this happens, provided one godparent is a confirmed Catholic, it is certainly allowable for a non-Catholic to act as a witness to the baptism as long as they are baptised and of sufficient age and maturity to understand their role.

STATE EDUCATION
There is an excellent school near our home. The Catholic school is some distance away and doesn't have a very good academic reputation. Must I send my son there?

All parents want to ensure that their children receive the best education possible. And the choice of school inevitably plays a major part in this, particularly at secondary level. Education is, of course, a much wider concept than simply what is learnt academically. It embraces attitudes, relationships and an overall preparation for life. Catholic schools aim to provide a good academic education within a totally Christian atmosphere. That is why Catholics prefer to send their children to Catholic schools where possible.

When a Catholic school is failing to provide a good academic education or where distance makes travelling difficult, parents are under no obligation to send their children to it. What they must ensure, though, is that the religious education of their child is not neglected. In many families this means that the parents must undertake it themselves. If you decide to send your child to a non-Catholic school, your Catholic partner will have to be prepared to teach your child about the faith at home.

HOME PRAYER
What is meant by "family prayer"?

Family prayer is a time when the family spend a few moments together thanking God for their lives and his gifts to them. It is a time when they also pray for any special needs they may have. These prayers are not meant to be lengthy or very formal in style or language. They are simply a reminder of unity and love within the Christian family. The best time for such prayers is when everyone is present, perhaps at the youngest child's bedtime or just after the evening meal.

CATHOLIC SCHOOLS
By sending children to denominational schools, don't we increase misunderstandings and division within our society?

Sadly, this is often the result of such schools. Their presence seems to fuel bigotry and suspicion. Yet at the heart of Christianity lies the firm belief that all men and women are of equal value and share equally in the love of God. A good Christian school should be able to convey this important point to its pupils. In a denominational school a child will also learn about the traditions, customs and beliefs of the particular religious "family" he or she belongs to. This should enhance and broaden understanding and promote a sense of mutual respect for other faiths.

WORSHIP TOGETHER
I am a practising Anglican and my husband is a Catholic. Is he allowed to attend my church regularly?

Yes, he is. In a mixed marriage, where both parties are practising members of different denominations, attendance at each other's church can be an important part of the sharing and the unity which is at the heart of the marriage. At present sharing communion between Christians is not generally permitted so neither of you is free to receive Holy Communion in the other's church. But there is no reason why your Catholic partner should not attend your church as long as he fulfils his obligations as a Catholic.

INTERCHURCH MARRIAGES

The Association of Interchurch Families was formed in 1968. Its aim is to provide help and support to marriages in which the partners are committed members of different Churches.

The Association offers such couples the opportunity to share their experiences and to talk over problems with people in a similar situation.

The Association has grown considerably since its foundation and there is now a network of regional groups. A biannual newsletter is sent to members and the Association also provides a useful advisory service.

For further information write to:
Association of InterChurch Families, Bastille Court, 2 Paris Garden London SE1 8ND

THE POPE AND MIXED MARRIAGES

Pope John Paul II visited Britain from 28th May to 2nd June 1982. One of the events during his visit was a service for the family, held at the Knavesmire racecourse in York. During his address on that occasion Pope John Paul had this to say:

"In your country, there are many marriages between Catholics and other baptised Christians. Sometimes these couples experience special difficulties. To these families I say: You live in your marriage the hopes and difficulties of the path to Christian unity. Express that hope in prayer together, in the unity of love. Together invite the Holy Spirit of love into your hearts and into your homes. He will help you to grow in trust and understanding. Brothers and sisters, 'May the peace of Christ reign in your hearts...let the message of Christ in all its richness, find a home with you' [Col. 3:15-16]."

Most people's idea of prayer is a leftover from their childhood...

GOD BLESS AUNTIE NELLIE AND UNCLE BERT...

In those days prayer was mainly about asking for things...

...AND SEND ME A BIKE FOR MY BIRTHDAY

So God seemed to be a sort of celestial Santa Claus...

HO, HO, HO!

The trouble was, he didn't always deliver the goods.

NO, NO, NO!

That's one reason why many people, as they grow older, abandon prayer altogether. Others continue to pray but often it remains more or less on the same childish level. In other words they still think of prayer primarily as a way of putting pressure on God to grant their requests.

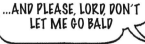

...AND PLEASE, LORD, DON'T LET ME GO BALD

At the root of this way of praying is an image of God as an extra-powerful man-in-the-sky, who needs to be kept informed about his world, so that he can take the necessary steps to iron out any problems.

OH LORD, AS YOU MAY HAVE SEEN ON NEWS AT TEN...

In sections two and three, we tried to show that this is not a very helpful way of thinking about God. Jesus talked about God in quite different terms – as a loving Father who already knows our needs. And it's this way of thinking about God that's at the heart of true prayer.

LOOK AT WHAT JESUS SAID IN ST MATTHEW'S GOSPEL

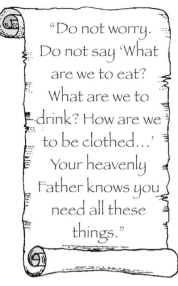

"Do not worry. Do not say 'What are we to eat? What are we to drink? How are we to be clothed...' Your heavenly Father knows you need all these things."

True prayer is rooted in the belief that God is with us. He is on our side, he is close to us, and he loves us. Catholics are encouraged to pray frequently. Not only when they're in church, but at other times as well: at home or out walking or in a favourite quiet place.

IT'S A COMPLETE WASTE OF TIME IF YOU ASK ME

In a way, you're not far wrong. Prayer has been called "wasting time with God". And that's an apt description. It's a bit like people in love.

WELL, WE JUST LIKE BEING TOGETHER

They don't feel the need to be constantly telling each other things, or even talking at all. They like being together just for its own sake.

It's the same with prayer. At its heart prayer is a relationship. It's simply wanting to be with God. As one holy old man put it when he was asked how he prayed...

HE LOOKS AT ME, AND I LOOK AT HIM

So prayer isn't measured by results. It's worthwhile for its own sake.

But very often people do speak to God when they pray. They express their thanks, their adoration, their sorrow for sin, their trust. And they ask for things, too. They know God doesn't need information, and they don't expect him to wave a magic wand to give them what they want. But by asking they acknowledge their complete dependence on God for everything.

Give us this day our daily bread...

People who pray frequently tend to speak to God on very familiar terms. They don't feel the need to use the sort of language you sometimes hear in church.

DEIGN, WE BESEECH THEE, ALMIGHTY GOD...

Instead they use their own words, and say what they want to say sincerely and honestly. Sometimes that means grumbling at God if they're angry or disappointed.

LORD, I'M THOROUGHLY SICK OF RELIGION

ME TOO

And there's nothing wrong with that if that's how you feel.

Another thing people discover when they pray is that the initiative doesn't come from them. God isn't waiting for people to pray to him, like someone at the other end of a telephone line...

DEAR, OH DEAR... THERE'S SOME BORING STUFF COMING UP TODAY

It's the other way round. The initiative comes from **God**. God is present to us all the time. God is to be found in **this** world: in the natural world around us, in other people, and at the deepest centre of our **own** being. When anyone prays they are opening themselves to the God who is already there and who continually offers himself to them.

THAT'S ALL VERY WELL, BUT ISN'T THIS PRAYER BUSINESS JUST ESCAPISM?

Actually it's just the opposite. People who seriously pray regularly cannot live on a trivial level. In prayer they explore the depth of their lives; they discover more clearly who they are and what their place in the world is. In prayer they open themselves and unite themselves to the love which is the source of all reality, and learn to share that love with others.

"The purpose of prayer is to meet God.
We are not really praying unless we are aware of being in his
presence and seeing our world and ourselves with his eyes.
To try to do this by escaping from the world or from people might be
trying to escape from God."

- Hubert Richards

"Prayer enlarges the heart until it is capable of containing
God's gift of himself."

- Mother Teresa

GOD KNOWS
If God knows everything, why should we pray for our needs?

We pray for our needs because we need to, not because God doesn't know our needs. God is continually inviting us to accept his gifts and his love, but we often fail to recognise this. Through prayer we grow increasingly conscious of God's care for us and we learn to respond to God's invitation. We begin to see our dependence and draw closer to him. Our prayer shows us where we stand before God. If we simply ask for things in prayer then we are childishly trying to use God as a slot machine. If we share our life, our feelings and our experiences with him we are setting the scene for a deep relationship based on loving trust.

In such a relationship there is no need for a request list. It's replaced by the confidence that our heavenly Father knows what is best for us. God anticipates our prayer and takes it into account. God knows our hearts and he can unite his gifts with their real need.

THE DEPARTED
What's the use of praying for the dead?

Catholics pray for the dead because they believe we are all part of the one family of God. This means being concerned about each other. This concern and unity is expressed when we pray for those who have died. We can't judge anyone's state before God, because we only see outside appearances. So when someone dies, Catholics pray for them that they may be completely reconciled to God in peace and eternal life. Such prayers also help those who are bereaved, for they experience the loving concern of their fellow Christians, which can help and heal at this difficult time.

PRAYING TO MARY
Why do Catholics pray to the mother of Jesus? Why can't they pray directly to God?

Catholics can, and do, pray directly to God. They also address prayers to Mary, the mother of Jesus. But they do not pray to Mary in the same way that they pray to God. Prayer to God is worship, and worship can be offered to God alone. Catholics do not worship Mary. When they address her in prayer it is to ask her to pray to Jesus for them. There's nothing unusual about that. We often ask our relatives or friends to pray for us. Catholics believe that, because of her special relationship to Jesus and the part she played in co-operating with God to make our salvation possible, Mary's intercession is particularly valuable.

At the marriage feast at Cana (narrated in the second chapter of John's Gospel) it was Mary who told Jesus, "They have no wine." And this prompted Jesus to work his first miracle. In the same way, Catholics ask her to make their needs known to Jesus.

Catholics look upon Mary as their spiritual mother, but the honour they show her does not arise from her own merits but from the special relationship she has with Jesus, her son.

EMBARRASSING REQUEST
Sometimes my wife suggests that we pray together, but I find the idea embarrassing. Do I have to agree?

Prayer is a very personal experience and it is most important that you feel relaxed and comfortable with it. There are as many ways of praying as there are people, and no one way is better or worse than another. Many Christians do like to share their prayer, to pray together. But probably just as many prefer to pray privately. So prayer within the family is very much a matter of personal choice. Some Catholic couples pray together, others do not. It is up to the individuals concerned to feel free to do what suits them best.

In making her suggestion your wife probably hopes that by sharing your prayer you and she will grow closer together. She is, no doubt, anxious that you shouldn't feel "cut off" from her by her religious beliefs. Tell her honestly how you feel whilst recognising and appreciating her thoughtfulness.

IDOLATRY
Why do Catholics pray to statues, crucifixes and holy pictures? Isn't this idolatry?

Catholics use statues, crucifixes and holy pictures as a focus for their prayer to remind them of what Christ has done for all of us, or to bring to mind a saint of the Church whose life is worthy of imitation. They do not pray to statues or pictures and they do not worship them.

Just as people keep photos and mementoes of someone they love, so Catholics like to have objects which remind them of Jesus, or Mary, or the saints. We are flesh-and-blood people, not disembodied spirits; and physical objects can be very helpful reminders of the spiritual side of our nature. Admittedly the use of statues and pictures can be exaggerated and in some places this might even verge on superstition. But such abuses are frowned on by the Church, and they do not reflect the attitude of most Catholics towards these visual aids.

THE ROSARY
What's the use of just repeating the same old words over and over again as Catholics do when they say the Rosary or some of their other prayers?

The repeated prayer is an aid to concentration. It's hard to sit still and think about God. Distractions and anxieties crowd in. Repeating a short prayer helps to focus attention and to still the mind. It is rather like a small child who rocks on her mother's lap murmuring, "Mummy, Mummy." She is concentrating on being with her mother, the words simply exercise that concentration. The use of a mantra in some Eastern religions serves a similar purpose.

WHY PRAY TO THE SAINTS

A Christian without a community is a contradiction in terms. Christians are essentially a family of believers. They become members of that family when they are baptised – and that is the original meaning of the word "saint". It simply meant "baptised". As time went on the word "saint" came to refer to those Christians who led lives of outstanding holiness and who were remembered and honoured after their deaths.

When Catholics talk about "the communion of saints" they are using the word "saint" in its original meaning. They mean all the baptised – those who are alive now and those who have departed from this world and now live on with Christ. Death does not destroy our union with Christians who have gone before us. We remain members of one family because we all share the life of Christ. That is why Catholics feel able to ask the saints in heaven to pray for them.

We've now had a look at the central beliefs of Catholics and told you about some of the things Catholics do as a result of those beliefs. In this final section we're going to build up a portrait of a Catholic by conducting an interview with our friend Fred – who you may remember we met in section five. (Yes, he **is** a Catholic!)

Fred, you don't mind being interviewed do you?

> Not in the least. As long as you don't mind me getting on with a bit of gardening while we're talking.

Fine. Well let's begin by asking you what effect your Catholic faith has on your life?

> I think it helps me make sense of my life. It gives me a sense of meaning and purpose. It helps me to see what's important and what isn't.

In section five we heard about a disastrous episode in your life when you were trying to be a Top Executive and it nearly wrecked your marriage. Where does your faith fit into that?

> I wish you hadn't reminded me of that. It was a very painful experience. But looking back, it was the best thing that could have happened to me.

> It taught me something about myself and I've been much happier and more contented since.

Did you think of it in any way as a religious experience?

> Not at the time. But looking back on it now, I think I **do** see the hand of God in it. Or rather, the **foot** of God… He was giving me a well-deserved kick in the pants. I suppose for me it was a kind of conversion.

And your wife, Sue, had a lot to do with it, didn't she?

> Yes, she did. She had every justification for walking out on me for good. But she didn't. She stood by me. That's what saved me really.

Now Sue isn't a Catholic, is she? So when you say you see the hand of God in that incident, do you think God was working through her?

> Yes, I do. I don't think Catholics have a sort of special claim on God. And I don't think God has to work through what you might call "official channels". God can work in any way he wants. And he does.

That incident obviously had a big effect on you. Do you think it's made you a better Catholic?

> Well, it's made me a better **person** – and I think that's the important thing. But a better Catholic? I don't know… I don't think in those sorts of terms any more.

But at one time you did, is that what you're saying?

> Yes, I suppose I am. The way I was brought up you measured your faith by external things: whether you went to Mass on Sundays, how frequently you went to Confession and Communion – all that sort of thing.

> I still think all that's very important. But it's not an end in itself. The important things go on **inside** you and no one can measure those.

Can you enlarge on what you meant when you said you think you're a better person?

> That's a difficult one. I don't mean I'm a paragon of virtue. I mean I'm a more complete person **in one respect**. That business about wanting to be a top executive: it was stupidity really, plus a lot of pride and a bit of envy. I discovered I wasn't that sort of person, and it was crazy to try to be.

So I learned something about myself and I've been more content since then. In **that** respect I'm a "better" person. But there are plenty of other things in my life that haven't changed for the better at all. So I don't think "I've made it". There's still a long way to go.

Do you mean God might have another big kick in the pants waiting for you?

Well, it's possible. I think we need to change many times if we're to be what God wants us to be, the people we **can** be. It might take a kick in the pants on occasion, but I think most of the time it's a gradual process – a process of growth.

Do you ever have any doubts about your faith?

I do find myself questioning certain beliefs from time to time. There was a programme on TV not long ago about the historical evidence for the life of Jesus…

That raised a few questions in my mind. But that's about **belief** rather than **faith**.

Is there a difference?

I think there is. On Sundays at Mass we say the Creed: "We believe in one God" and all that. Now I **believe** the statements of the Creed. But that's not what my **faith** is about. My faith isn't concerned with statements **about** God, it's concerned with God himself.

It's important to try to get the statements right, but you can never tie God down.

Do you mean your faith can change?

I think I'd say it **grows** rather than changes – in the same way that love grows. I remember my mother used to say: "Thank God we've got the faith" – as though we kept it in a box like the best cutlery.

But I don't think of faith as something I **have**. It's more a way of being.

Does that way of looking at it make life easier or more difficult?

Well it certainly makes it more unpredictable. And a bit risky, I suppose. But I thnk it's **meant** to be risky. After all, when Jesus said to Peter and the others: "Follow me" he didn't promise them an easy life, or instant answers to all their questions.

They were very much stepping into the unknown. I think it's the same for anyone who follows Christ.

But doesn't the Church tell you what to believe and what to do?

The Church **does** teach, yes; and that's vitally important. Without the Church I wouldn't know anything about Jesus at all. But the Church can't live my life for me. Somewhere along the line I've got to take responsibility myself.

continued

So the Church is a sort of guide?

Well, no. . . it's more than that. Saying it's a guide puts it **outside** me: something I **look** to. It's not like that. I'm **part** of the Church. I belong to a community of people who are trying to follow Jesus.

In recent years Catholics have talked of the Church being on a pilgrimage… a journey toward God; I like the image of us helping each other along the road as I need all the help I can get.

It also means we can only travel as fast as the stragglers. The front-runners have to wait for the slobs. That's a great consolation.

And presumably it's not only important that you are helped by **others**, but that you have to help **them** as well?

Oh, yes. That's fundamental. We've got to love other people and put that love into action.

It's not just Catholics you've got to love?

No, of course not. We've got to love everyone.

Do you **talk** about your beliefs very much?

Hardly at all. This interview is very unusual for me. I'm not very good at explaining my beliefs, and I can't say I like getting into arguments about religion.

Would you say your religion makes a big difference to your life?

Er… yes and no. I don't think it makes a big difference externally – I'm not running round to church or saying prayers all day long. But I think it **does** make a difference to the way I think about myself and other people… and to the way I treat other people. I hope it does, anyway.

Can you explain what that difference is?

It's hard to put into words. It's a sort of instinct that there's more to life than meets the eye; that we're here for a purpose; that you've got to take your own life, and other people's lives, seriously.

My faith keeps hauling me back from continually trying to live my life on a very trivial level.

Finally, Fred, could you try to put into words the essence of your Catholic faith as you see it?

I believe God loves us. Everything else flows from that.

"Jesus called the children to him and said, 'let the little children come to me, and do not stop them; for it is to such as these that the kingdom of God belongs. I tell you solemnly anyone who does not welcome the kingdom of God like a child will never enter it.'"
— Gospel of Luke: 18:15-17

EVERYDAY LIFE

What difference will it make to my everyday life being married to a Catholic?

The majority of Catholics are fairly sane and normal beings and their everyday lives do not differ noticeably from those of their neighbours. Their commitment to follow Jesus Christ does not involve "strange goings on"! It is a commitment to live as friends and followers of Jesus precisely within the context of daily life. In other words, their faith is not something "added on" to life, but is their life. That doesn't mean they are plaster saints – far from it. Like everyone else Catholics have their ups and downs, their successes and failures. But they do try to live according to the teachings of Jesus – especially his primary teaching to love one another. Your main source of puzzlement is likely to be why your partner can't put that into practice a bit more effectively.

INCREDIBLE BELIEFS

Why do Catholics believe things they know can't possibly be true?

Catholics have great confidence that their beliefs are true because those beliefs are based on a sound, rational foundation. Not all Catholics are expert theologians or specialists in Church history, so they may not be able to provide pat answers and proofs to every question about their religion. But it is a mistake to think that to have religious beliefs means you are gullible.

COMPLICATED FAITH

The Catholic faith seems very complicated. Will I be expected to know all its doctrines and its rules and regulations?

It's true that the Catholic faith can appear very complicated to someone who is unfamiliar with it. But Catholics themselves do not think of it as a long list of doctrines to be learned and a big book of rules to be obeyed. The central beliefs of Catholics do not differ from those of other Christians and it's these central beliefs that are at the heart of the Catholic faith, and that most Catholics "carry round with them".

The central beliefs of Catholics can be summarised like this: God has made himself known and given himself to us in the person of Jesus Christ. Jesus died on the cross to save us from sin and win forgiveness for us. He rose from death and lives on now, through his Spirit, in the community of believers which is the Church. As his followers we are to walk in his way by living lives of love and service.

All the other doctrines and practices of the Church fall into place round those central doctrines and take their meaning from them. Strictly speaking, you are not obliged to learn anything about the Catholic faith at all. But if you're aware of the basic doctrines outlined above you'll find that you'll gradually become familiar with other aspects of Catholic belief just through mixing with Catholics. So there's no need for you to "do a course" or anything like that! But whether you learn anything or not is entirely up to you.

TWO REAL-LIFE STORIES

Two couples talk about their experience of marriage. In each case one of the partners is a Catholic and the other is not.

Tom and Sue have been married for fifteen years. Tom is not a Catholic. They have two children, Mark who is thirteen and Helen who is seven. Tom and Sue went out together for about three years before they became engaged and they both feel that this gave them quite a lot of time to sort out their ideas and attitudes about all sorts of things including religion.

Tom feels quite strongly about a number of Catholic attitudes: "As a non-Catholic you seem to be expected to subjugate your views to the Church," he says. "I didn't have any strong religious convictions so this was not too difficult and I came to terms with it, but there is this powerful expectation that you will comply in certain matters, particularly in relation to the children. This is something you have to come to terms with; you must be prepared to compromise."

Tom would not describe himself as a "religious person", but he has no problem in understanding the basic Christian beliefs of his Catholic wife. It is what he calls the "extras" which still puzzle him. "I can't understand papal infallibility, confession, intercession to the saints or worship of the Virgin Mary. It's difficult if you're not a Catholic to express your views on these matters to children until they are older. I didn't want to put ours through the turmoil of challenging their beliefs. They need consistency; but it's hard always suppressing your own views. It can put a strain on the marriage, and this is where it's important for the Catholic to be supportive and not allow a kind of blackmail to creep into the family which pressurises Daddy to go to Mass or whatever."

Sue has found a useful counterbalance to this problem in being part of the Christian community rather than simply attending church on Sunday. Their children go to the Catholic school and belong to the scouts and brownies. Tom helps with the scouts and is on the parents' committee at the school. In this way he is very much part of the community without having compromised his own religious beliefs.

Sue does admit to feeling rather alone in terms of family prayer or worshipping together: "It's rather like having a sport which everyone in the family is crazy about apart from one person. It's difficult for everyone because you're not totally together. I also find it difficult, when we're away on holiday or visiting friends, to have to go in search of a Catholic church for Sunday Mass. But I feel I must keep my own standards otherwise you just fall away; it's so easy to do that in a mixed marriage."

Both Tom and Sue feel that their strength lies in the ability to accept each other's point of view and right to a personal belief without having to force it on their partner. Their early days of talking through possible difficulties have helped them in almost every area. Tom cannot accept or understand the Catholic attitude to artificial contraception and says so. But he does agree with the Church's stand against abortion. This illustrates, he feels, the importance of the Catholic partner being willing to show tolerance and flexibility.

One of their original problems was facing some of the ideas Tom's family had about Catholics. Sue recalls: "One elderly aunt asked, 'Do you sing carols?' And a number had misgivings about a wedding in a Catholic church. Would it all be in Latin? Would there be loads of statues? Would everyone keep crossing themselves? It's important to be prepared for these ideas, which sound strange to many Catholics, and be willing to answer queries openly and honestly.

"When you meet someone and fall in love with them you don't think about the consequences of that person having different religious views. But you do need to sort out things before you marry, particularly your ideas about children. If you are marrying someone who isn't a Catholic, it can be a good thing for your marriage because you are both forced to look at yourselves a little harder and with a little more tolerance and good humour!"

Bill and Angela have been married for seven years. They have two children, John aged four and Emily who is two. Bill, the Catholic partner, teaches at the local Catholic school. Angela belongs to the Church of England, though she is not actively involved in her present parish.

Bill recalls how he felt when he realised he wanted to marry Angela: "I was tremendously worried. I went through hell. I think I was ultra-sensitive because of my position in the local Catholic school. I felt it carried certain expectations and extra pressures. I wondered if these would cause extra strain on our marriage and whether I was being fair to Angela.

"I wondered what my family would say, but in the event that was a needless anxiety. The fact that she was the girl I wanted to marry meant that they accepted her immediately, regardless of religious beliefs."

Angela was not so anxious at the time: "I had no pre-conceived ideas about Catholics," she says. "I remembered that as a child the Catholics went to a different school from the rest of us. And then, when I was older, I recalled that Catholics I had met didn't seem any different from anyone else except that they tended to disappear for Mass on Sundays.

"I didn't find the marriage preparation talks difficult because we had already got to know the priest so it was like seeing a friend. I do have difficulties with Catholic ideas about the Virgin Mary. When I pray I don't feel the need to go to God through anyone else! I regarded family planning, then and now, as my problem so that hasn't been a difficulty. I was quite happy to be married in the Catholic church because I was already familiar with it and I knew how important it was to Bill.

"Bill was already totally committed to his religion when I first met him so I recognised how important his faith was to him. I think the fact that my own father is a practising Anglican helped me to understand Bill's feelings in religious matters.

"Although Bill has always gone to Mass regularly, he is very good at making sure it doesn't disrupt our family life. We go to Mass as a family once a month. I enjoy it, though it's rather difficult to keep track of the children at times. At Mass I feel very stupid, though, because I don't know the words of the Creed or the Gloria off by heart when everyone else seems to. Sometimes I mouth the words! It's silly really and I suppose I must learn them for the children's sake."

Bill is very appreciative of Angela's interest and support and recognises what a difference it makes to his life as a Catholic: "We say a few simple prayers together with the children each evening after bath time and their story. One evening Angela says a prayer, the next evening I do – nothing very elaborate, usually something we've made up which the children can relate to. Then the children join in as best they can.

"I never pray that Angela will become a Catholic. I do pray that if it should be for her spiritual good that we will see that and she might then become one. Deep down, of course, I would love her to become a Catholic but it would have to be for her sake, not mine.

"Occasionally, when I see Catholic families all going to Communion together, I think it would be nice if we were like that. But then I think, well, maybe those people haven't got the quality of relationship that we have. Maybe their faith doesn't mean as much to them. I do know that even if Angela never becomes a Catholic I would have no regrets about our marriage."

MEMO BOARD

MOST OF THE THINGS YOUR CATHOLIC PARTNER BELIEVES ARE THINGS ALL CHRISTIANS BELIEVE – OF WHATEVER CHURCH.

Have a sense of humour about religious matters. Catholics are not puritanical and they don't usually mind a joke at their own expense.

Don't imagine that you have nothing to contribute to your partner's spiritual well-being.

Being a Catholic doesn't stop people being weak, stupid or sinful. So don't expect your Catholic partner to be a saint.

Your partner is not an expert on Catholicism. Most Catholics know what they believe, but they haven't got the answer to every possible question at their fingertips.

Try to be sensitive to the special times in your children's religious development – like first Holy Communion.

Tell your partner about your strongly held beliefs, ideals and values.

Tell your partner if you think his or her Catholic beliefs are interfering with your marriage.

Notes for Catholics...

Make a serious effort to understand your partner's beliefs – and respect them.

Don't give your children the impression that you are superior to your partner in religious matters.

If your partner is a member of another Church, try to attend services with him or her whenever it's appropriate.

REFRAIN FROM PRESSURISING YOUR PARTNER INTO JOINING IN CATHOLIC PRACTICES IF HE OR SHE IS RELUCTANT TO DO SO.

Don't be tempted to think you know everything about religion and your partner knows nothing.

The History Game

Rules:
1. Any number of people can play.
2. You have to be willing to take a few knocks.
3. Use one dice.
4. You must throw the exact number to finish.

1
You learn that Jesus is risen from the dead. You are ready to start.

2

3

4
Year: 67
Peter is crucified in Rome. If you land with a martyr next turn take an extra turn. If you land in a catacomb go forward 2 spaces.

5 Catacomb

6
Year: 107 IGNATIUS (Martyr)

7

8
Year: 165 JUSTIN (Martyr)

9 Catacomb

10
Year: 258 CYPRIAN (Martyr)

11

12
Year: 300
You seek refuge in desert with St Antony and the desert fathers. It's a hidden life so **miss your next turn**.

13

14

15
Year: 313
Edict of Milan. Roman Emperor becomes a Christian. You become a member of the official religion.
Go forward 4 spaces.

16

17

18
Go back 2 spaces. Many deny that Jesus is God. Question settled at Council of Nicaea in year 325.

19

20

21
Athanasius, a great teacher in the Church. Take an extra turn if you land on this or ANY blue square.

22

23
Year: 397 AMBROSE

24

25
Year: 420 JEROME

26

27
Year: 430 AUGUSTINE

28

29

30
Year: 300-500
The Roman Empire is breaking up. But you have landed with the Celtic Church which kept faith alive in isolated areas. **Take an extra turn.**

31

32
Year: 432
St Patrick in Ireland.

33

34 - Year: 547
You become a monk in a newly founded monastery of St Benedict. You help to give stability to society. **Take an extra turn.**

35
Year: 590 GREGORY

36

37
Year: 597
St Augustine lands in Britain with 40 monks. Add 4 to your next score.

38

39

40
Year: 730
St Bede, a great scholar of the Church in Britain, includes you in his book on the history of the Church.
Take an extra turn.

41
Year: 754
You are a witness to the violent martyrdom of St Boniface, a great missonary from Devon. You are delayed in Germany.
Miss 1 turn.

42

43

44
Year: 800
Pope Leo crowns Charlemagne as "Roman Emperor". Church and State try to work together. If your throw was an odd number go back 5 spaces; if an even number go forward 4 spaces.

45

46
Year: 846
You are in Rome when it is under attack. **Miss a turn.**

47

48

49
Year: 870
Dispute between Photius and the Pope, to lead to the greatest schism in the Church between East and West. You don't know which way to turn, so miss 2 turns.

50
A "Dark Age" for the Church. If you land on a red section next time, **miss a turn.**

51

52

53

54

55
Year: 930
Odo reforms monasteries beginning with Cluny.
Go forward 2 spaces.

56
Year: 1000
Many await the end of the world, but remain disappointed.
Miss 1 turn.

76

75

74
Year: 1400
Church is in a mess: three men claim to be Pope. If you are a man miss 1 turn; if you are a woman take an extra turn.

73
Great Gothic cathedrals built.
Go forward 3 spaces.

72
Year: 1274 BONAVENTURE

71

70
Year: 1274 THOMAS AQUINAS

69

68
Year: 1215
The Inquisition is set up to punish heretics. If you have just thrown an odd number go back 4 spaces.

67

66
Year: 1210
You listen to a sermon preached by Francis of Assisi and wake up to the fact that the Church is going forward. **Move on 5 spaces.**

65

64
Year: 1170
Tensions grow between Church and State. Thomas Becket murdered in Canterbury. Christendom reels under the blow.
Go back 7 spaces

63

62

61
Year: 1147
St Bernard founds Cistercians but they are too strict for you.
Miss 1 turn.

60

59
Year: 1095 - 1272
You join the Crusades to win back the Holy Land.
These are difficult and confusing times.
Miss 1 turn.

77
Year: 1431
You help to burn Joan of Arc.
Go back 10 spaces.

78
Year: 1453
You are in Constantinople when the city is captured.
Schism between Eastern and Western Churches is total.
If you have just thrown a 6, go back to space 47.

79

80
Year: 1517
Martin Luther posts up "95 theses" - regarded as start of "Protestant Reformation". **Go back to where you have just come from.**

81

82
Year: 1545
Council of Trent. Church begins programme of self-reform.
If you land on a blue square next time, take an extra turn. If not, miss a turn.

83
Year: 1547
Thomas More beheaded in England. **Miss 1 turn.**

84
Year: 1550
St Ignatius founds Jesuits who take Gospel to new mission lands.

85
Year: 1555
Queen Mary in England puts Protestants to death. **Miss 1 turn.**

86
Year: 1560
St Teresa of Avila leads reform in prayer.

87
Year: 1570
Queen Elizabeth in England makes Catholics traitors to the State. **Miss 1 turn.**

88
Year: 1580
St Charles Borromeo reforms clergy.

89
Year: 1605
Gunpowder plot in England.
Miss 1 turn.

91
Year: 1622
Francis de Sales and Jane de Chantal found Visitation Sisters. Their writings emphasise God's love. **Take an extra turn.**

90

92

It's your lucky number
YOU'VE WON!

106
Year: 1962 - 65
Second Vatican Council helps to bring the Church up to date. And you are with it.
Go forward 1 space.

105

104
Year: 1900
You have just realised with St Therese of Lisieux (died 1897) that the important thing is to do small things well and with love.
Take an extra turn.

103
Year: 1858
You are one of the first to go on a pilgrimage to Lourdes where the Blessed Virgin appeared to Bernadette. **Take an extra turn.**

102

101
Year: 1840
"Oxford Movement" in England brings converts to Catholicism, helped by Emancipation of Catholics.
Catholic Church moves forward, as do you by 1 space.

100

99
Year: 1789
You escape with your head in French Revolution but lose your money in persecution against the Church. **Go back 9 spaces**

98

97

96
Year: 1732
St Alphonsus founds Redemptorists to preach to poor.
Go forward 4 spaces.

95
Year: 1680
John Baptist de la Salle founds teaching brothers.
Go forward 3 spaces.

94

93
Year: 1640
Jansenist heresy emphasises God's "anger". **Learn a lesson and go back 1 space.**

A DICTIONARY OF CATHOLIC TERMS

The following list is by no means exhaustive. But it includes many words and phrases you may well come across if you are married to a Catholic

A

Absolution: Part of the sacrament of reconciliation. It is the formal declaration by the priest that a penitent's sins are forgiven.

Abstinence: Refraining from certain kinds of food or drink as an act of self-denial. Usually, refraining from eating meat. Official days when Catholics abstain from eating meat are Ash Wednesday and Good Friday.

Advent: The season of the Church's year leading up to Christmas. It includes the four Sundays before Christmas and it is a time of preparation for the "coming" of Christ. Advent marks the beginning of the Church's year.

All Saints' day: The day on which Catholics remember all the saints of the Church, whether officially canonised or not. It is celebrated on November 1st.

All Souls' day: The day on which Catholics remember the dead and pray for them, recognising that they may still need to be brought to perfection. It is observed on November 2nd.

Altar: The table on which the sacrifice of the Mass is celebrated.

Angel: The word means "messenger". In the Bible they are described as carrying messages from God to human beings.

Angelus: A form of prayer said three times a day: in the morning, at noon and in the evening. When said in monasteries or churches it is customary to ring the bells.

Annunciation: The "announcement" by the angel Gabriel to Mary that she was to be the mother of the Saviour. The feast of the Annunciation is celebrated on March 25th.

Apostolate: The work of an apostle. It is used to describe any work, ministry or service which is carried out on behalf of the Church. For example, the apostolate of a religious order is the work the order undertakes.

Ascension: The taking up of Jesus into heaven forty days after the resurrection and witnessed by the apostles. Ascension Thursday is celebrated forty days after Easter.

Ash Wednesday: The first day of Lent. By tradition Catholics have ashes put on their foreheads on this day as a mark of repentance. They also fast on this day and abstain from eating meat.

Assumption: The taking up of Mary the mother of Jesus into heaven. Catholics celebrate this on August 15th.

Ave Maria: Latin words meaning "Hail Mary", the first words of the most popular prayer Catholics address to Mary.

B

Beatification: The first step in the process by which a dead person is officially declared to be a saint.

Benediction: A short service in which the consecrated Host is placed in a monstrance where it can be seen and venerated by the people. At the conclusion of the service the priest blesses the people with the monstrance containing the Host.

Bidding prayers: Prayers which are said at Mass after the Creed for the needs of the Church and the world. Also referred to as "the prayer of the faithful".

Bishop: Someone ordained to be principal shepherd in the Church, a centre of unity.

Blessed Sacrament: A term Catholics use when referring to the consecrated Host – especially when it is reserved in the tabernacle.

Blessing: A short prayer, usually accompanied by the sign of the cross, asking God's favour on persons or objects.

Breviary: A book containing the prayers, hymns, psalms and readings which make up the Divine Office – traditionally the prayer of the Church said at various times during the day.

C

Canonisation: The official declaration by the Pope that a dead person is a saint and may be publicly venerated.

Canon law: The law of the Church.

Catechism: A written summary of Christian teaching, often in question-and-answer form.

Catechist: Someone who teaches Christian doctrine, especially in parish or school.

Celebrant: The one who presides at a religious service. The priest at Mass is referred to as the celebrant.

Chalice: The cup used at Mass to hold the wine.

Charismatic Renewal: A movement within the Church which aims for renewal by being attuned to the power of the Holy Spirit working in the lives of individuals and communities.

Chrism: A mixture of olive oil and balsam which is blessed by the bishop on Holy Thursday and is used in the administration of the sacraments of baptism, confirmation and holy orders.

Christmas: The feast of the birth of Jesus, celebrated on December 25th.

Christ the King: A feast celebrated on the last Sunday of the Church's year acclaiming Christ as king of the world.

Ciborium: A bowl or chalice-shaped vessel to hold the consecrated hosts for the distribution of Holy Communion.

Clergy: A term applied to men who have been ordained for ministry within the Church. Bishops, priests and deacons are members of the clergy.

Communion under both kinds: Receiving Holy Communion under both the forms of bread and wine. It is becoming increasingly common for Catholics to receive Holy Communion in this way, particularly on special occasions.

Concelebration: The celebration of Mass by several priests together.

Conclave: The meeting of the Cardinals, in complete seclusion, when they assemble to elect a Pope.

Confessor: A priest who hears confessions.

Consecration: Making something sacred. It describes the moment during Mass when the bread and wine are changed into the Body and Blood of Christ.

Contrition: The acknowledgement of sin and sorrow for it.

Convent: The place where a community of nuns lives.

Corpus Christi: A Latin phrase meaning "the Body of Christ". The feast of Corpus Christi commemorates the institution of the Eucharist and is celebrated on the Thursday after Trinity Sunday.

Creed: A summary of Christian beliefs.

Crucifix: A cross with the figure of the crucified Jesus upon it. Used by Catholics to bring to mind the sufferings of Christ.

C.W.L.: Stands for Catholic Women's League: an organisation which promotes religious education and social welfare and represents Catholic women's interests on national and international bodies.

D

Deacon: Someone ordained to minister within the Church. May preach and administer some of the sacraments.

Deanery: Several parishes form a deanery. This unit is administered by one of the priests of the deanery who has the title "Dean".

Devil: The biblical name for the evil one, a creature who rebelled against God and causes evil.

Diocese: An area under the care of a bishop.

Dispensation: Exemption from a Church law in a particular case for a special reason.

Doctrines: The beliefs of Catholics, expressed in the Creed and other official documents.

Dogma: Doctrines put forward by the Church which are to be accepted by Catholics as true and clear statements of belief.

E

Easter: The day on which Christians celebrate the resurrection of Jesus.

Ecumenism: The work for unity between the different Christian Churches.

Enclosure: That part of a convent or monastery to which outsiders are not admitted.

Encyclical: A letter from the Pope to the whole Church, usually dealing with matters of faith and the Christian life.

Epiphany: The feast which commemorates the visit of the wise men to the infant Christ in Bethlehem. It is celebrated on January 6th.

Eucharist: Literally means "Thanksgiving", another name for the Mass, the principal celebration of the Catholic community.

Excommunication: Cutting someone off from the community of the Church because of serious offences against its law or teaching. It is resorted to only rarely.

F

Fasting: Eating less food than usual as an act of self-denial. Catholics fast on Ash Wednesday and Good Friday.

Feast day: A day of special solemnity within the Church.

First Friday: See "Sacred Heart".

Font: A basin or bowl in a church used for the baptismal water.

Friday penance: In commemoration of the sufferings of Christ Catholics perform some act of self-denial every Friday. This used to take the form of abstaining from meat, but now Catholics may choose one of several forms of self-denial.

G

Genuflection: Kneeling on one knee as a sign of honour and worship to Jesus Christ and an expression of faith in his presence in the tabernacle under the form of bread. Catholics genuflect when entering and leaving a church.

Godparent: Someone who undertakes to ensure that a child who is baptised will be brought up in the Catholic faith. The godparent must be a Catholic, though he or she may be assisted by a godparent who is a member of another Christian Church.

Good Friday: The day on which the crucifixion of Jesus is commemorated. It is a day of special solemnity for Catholics. They fast and abstain from meat on this day.

Gospel: A word meaning "Good News". The proclamation of the good news of salvation won for us by Jesus Christ. The word is also used of the four books which tell of the life, death and resurrection of Jesus: the Gospels of Matthew, Mark, Luke and John.

Grace: The gift of God's love and help which is given to us freely, without any previous efforts on our part.

Grace at meals: A short prayer before and after meals thanking God for the food we eat and asking his blessing on those who have prepared it.

H

Habit: The distinctive form of dress worn by members of religious communities.

Hail Mary: The most popular prayer Catholics address to Our Lady. It derives from the angel's greeting (Luke 1:28) and the greeting of Mary's cousin Elizabeth (Luke 1:42) adding to these a request to Mary to pray for us. The full prayer is: Hail Mary, full of grace, the Lord is with thee; blessed art thou amongst women and blessed is the fruit of thy womb, Jesus. Holy Mary, mother of God, pray for us sinners now and at the hour of our death. Amen.

Heresy: A teaching which deviates from the accepted beliefs of the Catholic Church.

Hierarchy: The organisation of clergy according to the ranks of holy orders.

Holy Hour: A service in which Jesus is venerated in the Blessed Sacrament.

Holy Saturday: The day between Good Friday and Easter Sunday.

Holy Thursday: The day before Good Friday. On this day Catholics commemorate the supper Jesus had with his disciples on the night before he died.

Holy water: Water which has been blessed by a priest. Catholics sprinkle themselves with holy water as they make the sign of the cross on entering a church as a reminder of their baptism. Holy water is also used for blessings.

Holy Week: The final week of Lent, leading up to Easter Sunday. The last three days of Holy Week (Holy Thursday, Good Friday and Holy Saturday) are days of special solemnity.

Homily: see "Sermon".

Host: The wafer of consecrated bread which Catholics receive at Holy Communion. It is usually disc-shaped and thin for convenience, and there are two sizes – the larger is used by the priest at the altar.

I

Icon: A picture of Christ, Mary, or the saints painted in the style of the Eastern Church. Often painted on wood and adorned with precious stones.

Immaculate Conception: The doctrine that Mary was conceived without inheriting original sin. (Not to be confused with the virgin birth of Jesus.)

Impediment to marriage: Something which prevents a person entering into a church marriage. For example, certain degrees of blood-relationship between the partners, or where one partner is not baptised. A dispensation can be obtained from some impediments.

Incarnation: A theological term for the Son of God becoming man in Jesus Christ.

Indulgence: Remission of the punishment or penance due to sin after its guilt has been forgiven. By virtue of the authority given it by Christ, the Church may grant to those who have received forgiveness of their sins a share in the merits of Christ and the saints so that the burden of punishment their sins deserve may be removed or lightened. To gain an indulgence Catholics must be free from serious sin and must carry out the prescribed good works, or recite certain prayers, which the Church attaches to the indulgence.

Intercession: The prayers the saints in heaven offer to God on behalf of people on earth who request their help.

J

Jesus: There are a number of symbols for the name Jesus which you may see in churches or in works of religious art. These are some of them:

IHS: three letters from the Greek name, Jesus.

INRI: the initial letters from the Latin inscription written on the cross: "Iesus Nazarenus Rex Iudaeorum" (Jesus of Nazareth, King of the Jews).

PX: a monogram of the first two Greek letters for "Christos". A fish is also a symbol of Christ. The initial letters of the Greek word for fish, "Ichthus", stand for "Jesus Christ, Son of God and Saviour".

Joseph: The husband of Mary, venerated as a saint. His feast is celebrated on March 19th.

K

Kyrie eleison: Greek words meaning "Lord have mercy". Sometimes said or sung in Greek during the penitential rite of the Mass.

L

Laity: Members of the Church who do not belong to the clergy or to a religious order.

Last judgement: The judgement of every person by Jesus Christ at the end of time.

Last Supper: The supper Jesus had with his disciples on the night before he died, during which he instituted the Eucharist.

Lay apostolate: Work done on behalf of the Church by lay people.

Lectern: The stand from which the scriptures are read in church.

Lectionary: The book containing the scripture readings for Mass.

Lent: A period of six weeks leading up to Easter. It begins on Ash Wednesday and is a time of self-denial in preparation for Easter. Catholics usually choose some form of self-denial which they observe during Lent.

Litany: A form of prayer in which the priest recites a series of petitions to God, or calls on the help of the saints. These petitions are followed by a set response said or sung by the congregation.

Liturgical year: The worship of the Church over the period of a year during which the central mysteries of faith are unfolded. The chief festivals are Christmas, Easter and Pentecost.

Liturgy: The public worship of the Church.

Lord's Prayer: The prayer Jesus taught his followers to say: the "Our Father".

M

Magisterium: The teaching authority of the Church.

Martyr: A Christian who bears witness to the truth of the gospel to the point of death.

Mass: See "Eucharist".

Maundy Thursday: See "Holy Thursday".

May devotions: Special services held during the month of May to honour Mary, the mother of Jesus.

Meditation: Reflecting on God or the things of God in one's own heart.

Missal: A book containing the prayers of the Mass.

Missionaries: Christians who proclaim the gospel to non-Christians in a foreign country. It is also often applied to anyone who endeavours to share his or her faith with others.

Mixed marriage: A marriage between Christians of different denominations. Catholics need permission from the Church before they can contract such a marriage.

Monstrance: An ornate receptacle in which a consecrated Host is placed so that Jesus, in the form of bread, can be seen and venerated by the people.

Mortal sin: A serious sin by which a Christian cuts himself or herself off from God's grace. Catholics who are conscious of having committed a mortal sin are bound to confess to a priest.

Mother of God: A title given to Mary because she is the mother of Jesus who is both God and man.

Mystery: A truth which cannot be grasped by human reason.

N

New Testament: That part of the Bible which tells the Good News of Jesus Christ.

Novena: Nine days of prayer. It has its origin in the nine days the disciples spent in prayer awaiting the coming of the Holy Spirit, between the Ascension and Pentecost.

Novice: A person who has been accepted into a religious order and who is undergoing a period of training and formation before taking any vows.

Novitiate: The period a novice spends in training.

Nun: A member of an enclosed religious order of women. Members of orders which are not enclosed are usually referred to as religious sisters.

Nuptial Mass: A Mass which includes the wedding service. Not all weddings in the Catholic Church are accompanied by Mass. It is quite common to have the wedding service alone. There is no rule about this. The choice is up to the bride and groom.

O

Old Testament: That part of the Bible written before the time of Christ.

Ordination: The conferring of holy orders on a man, by which he becomes a bishop, priest or deacon.

Our Lady: The title Catholics most frequently use when referring to Mary, the mother of Jesus.

P

Pagan: A collective term meaning "unbelievers".

Palm Sunday: The Sunday before Easter. It commemorates the occasion when Jesus rode into Jerusalem on a donkey and the people waved palm branches in his honour. In the Catholic Church this Sunday is also called Passion Sunday.

Parables: The stories Jesus told which illustrate some of his most important teachings.

Paradise: Another word for heaven. It literally means "God's garden", and so is also used of the garden of Eden.

Parish: The community of the Church in a particular place.

Parish Council: A group of people elected by the parish who, together with the parish priest, look after various needs of the parish.

Parish Mission: A period of spiritual renewal within a parish, usually conducted by one or more visiting priests over a period of a week or a fortnight.

Passion: The suffering and death of Jesus on the cross endured for our salvation.

Passion Sunday: See "Palm Sunday".

Pastoral care: The caring work of the Church, particularly that exercised by ordained ministers. "Pastor" means "shepherd".

Pastoral letter: A letter sent from a bishop to his diocese on a number of occasions during the year. Pastoral letters are usually read out to the people during the Mass.

Pax Christi: Literally "The peace of Christ". It is the name of an international Catholic movement for peace.

Penance: The sacrament of penance is the sacrament in which sins are forgiven, now known as Reconciliation. The word "penance" also refers to acts of self-denial. For example, fasting can be described as an act of penance.

Pentecost: Literally means "fifty days". It marks the day when the Holy Spirit came upon the apostles fifty days after the resurrection of Jesus. Also called Whit Sunday.

Petition: Asking God for our needs in prayer.

Pilgrimage: A journey to a holy place. Popular places of pilgrimage today include the Holy Land, Rome and Lourdes.

Postulant: A person who has applied to join a religious order and is waiting to be admitted.

Prayer of the faithful: See "Bidding prayers".

Preaching: The proclamation of the gospel, challenging the listener to make a commitment. "To preach" also means: "to deliver a sermon".

Preface: A part of the Mass leading up to the Eucharistic Prayer.

Presbytery: The house, often adjoining the church, where the priests of the parish live.

Priest: Someone who is ordained to minister within the Church. The main duties of the priest are preaching, celebrating Mass, administering the other sacraments and exercising a role of leadership within the Church.

Procession: A solemn walk for a religious purpose, usually accompanied by prayers and hymns. Processions are not as common nowadays as they once were, but they are still held occasionally. For example, May Processions in honour of Our Lady.

Profession: The taking of vows on joining a religious order.

Purgatory: A state in which the souls of the dead are purified and perfected in love before finally becoming one with God in heaven.

R

Readers: Those who read the scripture passages during Mass. Passages from the Old Testament or parts of the New Testament may be read by lay people (men and women). Passages from the Gospels are always read by a priest or deacon.

Real Presence: The phrase Catholics use to indicate their belief that Jesus is really present in the Eucharist under the forms of bread and wine.

Redemption: Being delivered from evil through the birth, life, death and resurrection of Jesus Christ.

Reformation: A movement for the reform of certain doctrines and practices of the Church which began in the 16th century and led to the division between Catholic and Protestant (or Reformed) Churches.

Religious order: Name given to communities of men or women dedicated to some specific mission. See "Vows".

Requiem: A Mass for the dead. It takes its name from the first word of the prayer with which the Mass begins. In Latin this is: "Requiem aeternam dona eis, Domine." (Lord, give them eternal rest.)

Responsorial Psalm: A psalm which is recited or sung after the first scripture reading at Mass. The congregation recites or sings a response after each verse.

Resurrection of the body: The doctrine that at the end of time the redeemed will rise, body and soul, from the dead and live with God for ever.

Revelation: God's disclosure of himself to humanity. The greatest revelation of God is Jesus Christ.

Rosary: A form of prayer reflecting on the main events in the life of Jesus and Mary, his mother. There are twenty of these events, called "mysteries", divided into four groups of five: Joyful, Light, Sorrowful and Glorious. The prayers which go with each mystery are: one Our Father; ten Hail Marys; one Glory be to the Father. Rosary beads are used to help count the prayers. The repetition of the prayer is an aid to concentration and is used in rather the same way that a mantra is used in some Eastern religions.

S

Sacramentals: Rites which have some resemblance to sacraments but were not instituted by Christ. An example of a sacramental is the use of holy water.

Sacred Heart: The heart of Jesus, pierced by a lance when he hung on the cross, is honoured as a sign of his love for all people. The feast of the Sacred Heart of Jesus is celebrated in June and there is a tradition among Catholics of honouring Jesus under this title on the first Friday of every month.

Sacristy: The room in the church where the priest vests for Mass and other services and where the sacred vessels are kept.

Saints: Members of the Church whose holiness of life is recognised after their deaths and who are venerated by the Church on earth. Before anyone is proclaimed as a saint (canonised) a process of careful investigation of his or her life is carried out.

Sanctuary lamp: A lamp which is kept burning in front of the tabernacle in Catholic churches as a sign and a reminder that Jesus is really present.

Seminary: A college where men are trained for the priesthood.

Sermon: A talk in which the word of God is explained. Also called a homily. Only people who have been commissioned by the bishop are allowed to give sermons: usually priests or deacons.

Sign of the cross: A formula Catholics use to bless themselves. It is made with the right hand by touching the forehead, the breast and the shoulders while saying the words: "In the name of the Father and of the Son and of the Holy Spirit. Amen." Catholics make the sign of the cross at the beginning of Mass, at the beginning of other forms of prayer, and sometimes when beginning an activity or at the start of a new day.

Soul: The spiritual element of a person's nature.

Stations of the Cross: A series of fourteen meditations on incidents in the suffering and death of Christ. Pictures of these fourteen scenes can be found round the walls of most Catholic churches.

S.V.P.: Stands for "Society of St Vincent de Paul": a society of men and women willing to undertake active charitable works.

Synod: A meeting of about two hundred bishops from all over the world representing their various countries. Usually held in Rome every three years.

T

Tabernacle: The safe in which the consecrated Hosts are kept. It is usually situated behind the main altar in the church or at a special side-altar.

Ten commandments: The rules of life delivered by God to Moses on Mount Sinai. They still form the basis of morality for Christians.

Theology: The study of things concerned with Christian faith and the leading of the Christian life.

Tradition: The teaching which has been handed down from the apostles of Jesus and which continues to be handed on by the Church in every age.

Transubstantiation: A word Catholics use to describe the way in which Jesus is present in the Eucharistic bread and wine.

Tridentine Mass: The Latin Mass authorised by the Council of Trent in the 16th century. It was the form of Mass used in the Western Church until 1969 when Pope Paul VI authorised the use of a revised rite of Mass which could be said in the language of the country.

Trinity Sunday: The Sunday after Pentecost. A day on which special honour is paid to the Blessed Trinity.

U

U.C.M.: Stands for "Union of Catholic Mothers", an organisation of Catholic married women for the preservation of faith and morals in the home.

V

Vatican: The official residence of the Pope in Rome. It also refers to the central government of the Church.

Venial sin: A sin which is not so serious that it requires the sacrament of penance for its forgiveness.

Vespers: The evening prayer of the Divine Office.

Vestments: Garments worn by the ministers of the Church when celebrating Mass or administering the sacraments. These include the alb – a long white tunic worn by all ministers; the chasuble – the main outer-garment of the priest when celebrating Mass; the stole – a type of scarf worn round the neck. The stole is worn by all clergy when administering the sacraments, as well as for Mass.

Viaticum: Holy Communion given to a person who is dying. The word means "provision for a journey", namely, the journey through death to life in the world to come.

Virgin birth: The doctrine that Mary remained a virgin both before and after the birth of Jesus, her son. This doctrine preserves the truth that Jesus was both God and man. He was "conceived by the Holy Spirit", meaning that his origin is wholly from God; he was "born of the virgin Mary", meaning that he is fully human.

Vocation: The calling to a life of love, service and holiness which is addressed to all Christians. The word is also commonly used in a narrower sense to refer to the calling to the priesthood or religious life.

Vows: Solemn promises of poverty, chastity and obedience which are made to God by members of religious orders. They can be temporary (binding only for a time) or perpetual (binding for life).

W

Whitsunday: another name for the feast of Pentecost which celebrates the coming of the Holy Spirit on the apostles. "Whit" means "white". In earlier times the newly baptised wore the white robes of baptism on this day.

Some useful addresses

Association of Separated and Divorced Catholics
c/o Cathedral House, 250 Chapel Street, Salford, M3 5LL
Tel: 0113 264 0638
www.asdcengland.org.uk
An association of Catholics who have been involved in separation or divorce. A useful advice service is offered covering both legal and practical matters. There is a network of local groups, and contacts are available on the web.

Border and Immigration Agency
Lunar House, 40 Wellesley Road, Croydon, CR9 2BY
Tel: 0208 253 6700
www.ind.homeoffice.gov.uk
Offers advice and information to any British subject wishing to marry a non-British subject, either resident or non resident in this country. (The rules are different for men and women so it is important to check where necessary.)

Catholic Marriage Care
Clitherow House, 1 Blythe Mews, Blythe Road, London, W14 0NW
Tel: 0207 371 1341
Email: info@marriagecare.org.uk
www.marriagecare.org.uk
Provides education for family life, marriage counselling and a medical advisory service. There are local centres throughout England and Wales.

Compassionate Friends
53 North Street, Bristol, BS3 1EN
Tel: 08451 23 23 04
Email: info@tcf.org.uk
www.tcf.org.uk
An association for parents who have been bereaved. Members offer help, support and advice for families after the death of a child. This association also has a useful library of books on the subject which are available on loan.

Families Need Fathers
134 Curtain Road, London, EC2A 3AR
Tel: 0207 613 5060
Helpline: 08707 607 496 (6pm–10pm)
Email: fnf@fnf.org.uk
www.fnf.org.uk
An association for fathers interested in maintaining contact with their children following divorce or separation. This association also supports fathers who are caring for their children alone.

Fertility UK
Bury Knowle Health Centre, 207 London Road, Headington, Oxford, OX3 9JA
www.fertilityuk.org
Provides information about the latest techniques in natural family planning and can provide local contacts.

The Grail Centre
125 Waxwell Lane, Pinner, Middlesex, HA5 3ER
Tel: 0208 866 2195
Email: grailcentre@compuserve.com
Organises family days, special courses and ecumenical events to help build Christian communities. Also produces a number of interesting publications.

Hyperactive Children's Support Group
71 Whyke Lane, Chichester, West Sussex, PO19 7PD
Tel: 01243 539966 (M, T, Th, F 10 am to 12 noon)
Email: hacsg@hacsg.org.uk
www.hacsg.org.uk
Offers advice and information for parents who have a hyperactive child.

Mind (National Association for Mental Health)
Granta House, 15-19 Broadway, Stratford E15 4BQ
Tel: 0208 519 2122
MindinfoLine: 0845 766 0163
Email: contact@mind.org.uk
www.mind.org.uk
Provides information and advice about any problem relating to mental illness or handicap. In addition the organisation publishes a number of useful booklets and leaflets on related subjects. Regional contact details are available on the web.

The Miscarriage Association
c/o Clayton Hospital, Northgate, Wakefield, W Yorks, WF1 3JS
Tel: 01924 200799
www.miscarriageassociation.org.uk
Offers advice and information for anyone suffering a miscarriage or wishing to help a woman in this situation.

Movement of Christian Workers
St Joseph's, Watford Way, London, NW4 4TY
Tel: 0208 203 6290
Email: mcworkers@aol.com
www.mcworkers.org
Promotes family and house groups to help people relate their faith to everyday life.

National Childbirth Trust
Alexandra House, Oldham Terrace, Acton, London, W3 6NH
Tel: 0870 770 3236
Email: enquiries@nct.org.uk
www.nct.org.uk
The centre for all information and advice about childbirth and maternity services.

Parentline Plus
520 Highgate Studios, 53-79 Highgate Road, London, NW5 1TL
Helpline: Freephone 0808 800 2222
www.parentlineplus.org.uk
Works to offer help and support through an innovative range of free, flexible, responsive services – shaped by parents for parents.

Pre-School Learning Alliance
The Fitzpatrick Building, 188 York Way, London, N7 9AD
Tel: 0207 697 2500
www.pre-school.org.uk
Provides a complete service for anyone involved in organising or setting up playgroups for under-fives.